PRAISE FOR *BE FEARLESS*

"Jane's book is a must read for professional women or for those aspiring to have a fulfilling career. Her essays are authentic and deal with real-world personal and professional issues many women face and provide solutions to or ways of thinking about those challenges. This book is also a must read for company leaders to gain insight into the way the culture within their institutions may be preventing them from benefiting from the full talents of the women within their organizations. Finally, it is a must read for partners of professional women, encouraging them to open their eyes and see whether they are enabling or stiffing the aspirations of those they love."

Joyce M. Roche
Author of *The Empress Has No Clothes: Conquering Self-Doubt to Embrace Success* and
Board member of Macy's Inc., Tupperware Corporation

"Jane has written a very compelling book that addresses many facets of building a successful career as a woman. The insights provided will be useful to women aspiring to move up the career ladder."

Funke Opeke
Chief Executive Officer, MainOne

"Jane's book is a must own and a must read for every woman, whether in the public or private sector. She has shown that with determination and hard work, destinies can change. Thanks, Jane, for speaking to all of us!"

Ambassador Folake Marcus – Bello
CEO/Principal Partner Folake Bello & co "The Godmother"

"Jane is an inspiring friend and impressive business leader, whose stories and tips will motivate anyone who reads her book."

Aliza Knox
Head of Cloudflare APAC

be fearless

GIVE YOURSELF PERMISSION TO BE YOU

JANE EGERTON-IDEHEN

ISBN: 978-1-7345732-0-6 (hardcover)
ISBN: 978-1-7345732-1-3 (paperback)
ISBN: 978-1-7345732-2-0 (ebook)

All illustrations by Smids Animation Studios http://smidsstudios.com.

Cover photograph by Kola Oshalusi

For more information, visit www.janeegerton.com

For bulk book orders, contact Jane Egerton-Idehen at Jane@ janeegerton.com.

Table of Contents

Dedication vii
Acknowledgements ix
Foreword xi
Introduction xv
Chapter 1: The Caged Bird 1
Chapter 2: I Have a Dream(I) 11
Chapter 3: I Have a Dream(II) 27
Chapter 4: The Corporate Escalator 35
Chapter 5: Egerton and I 45
Chapter 6: Motherhood and Birth Stories 55
Chapter 7: It is Lonely at the Top 65
Chapter 8: Women and Career 73
Chapter 9: Friends Incorporated 83
Chapter 10: Giving Yourself Permission 91
Chapter 11: Tea with the Men 103
Chapter 12: The Men's Roundtable 113
Chapter 13: Closing Thoughts 125
About the Author 129
References 133

Dedication

To Sarah, my daughter.
The moment I first held you in my hands, I knew
I would have to share my story.

Acknowledgements

This book originated with a series of articles in which I shared my career experiences and journey with others. My goal was to help people on their own journeys by sharing things that I had learned along the way. The writing also served a therapeutic purpose during a challenging time of my life. I am grateful for the opportunity to help others thrive and be empowered.

I thank Eleanor Chin for insisting that I turn the articles into a book. She always believed that I had much to give to others. For those articles, Joanna Bamfo was my editor, and she ensured that my work was professional. In addition, Timi Yeseibo worked with me tirelessly over a year to help me produce this book. Her amazing professionalism and work ethic made sure that my dream came true.

I want to acknowledge all the wonderful people who allowed me to share their stories, including Gloria, Gifty, Magnus, Aficanus, Lucy, and Chinwe. My hope is that your stories serve as a source of great inspiration and knowledge for readers of this book.

A huge part of this book would have been incomplete without my friends. Thank you to Phyllis Kuenyehia and Hilda Haggar Ampadu. Friendships that started in Ghana became a sisterhood. Many of the ideas in this book began with our discussions and brainstorming about our careers. Such talks with friends have impacted me positively and strengthened my soul. To my dear sisters, Lynda Saint Nwafor and Ugonwa Nwoye, "Daaalu rine."

The greatest sacrifice while I worked on this book was made by my magnificent family. I am so grateful to Egerton, Asher, and Sarah, who supported me and gave me the space I needed during those late nights and early mornings to write and rewrite. Your love and belief in me gave me the wings to fly.

Foreword

Uncaged!

The two words that come to mind when I think of Jane are joy and tenacity.

I first met Jane a few years ago when she invited me to the International Women's Day celebration for undergraduates hosted by Ericsson Ghana.

Since Ericcson was one of our telecom vendors at the time, accepting the invitation to speak to this group of young girls was easy. What I hadn't bargained for was meeting Jane, along with the other amazing women she had invited.

Jane turned out to be this amazing beam of light who was clearly passionate about mentoring these young women. This was not a woman fulfilling a corporate duty – she was a woman on a mission to ensure that young women are able to find their place and their voices through the inspiration of the invited speakers.

Jane exudes joy in all that she does. A joy borne out of her confidence in who she is and what she is purposefully working to achieve.

As we work together to create African prosperity, the narrative that is the African woman's experience needs to come to the fore. Yes, the stories vary, and that is exactly why the story of Jane being uncaged is an important one to hear. We have to hear more varied stories of experiences of African woman building all facets of their lives. The ups and downs. The joys and tears. The challenges and lessons learnt. It is by hearing more stories told authentically by the people who live the African experience will we appreciate what it takes to see our women succeed. Understanding factors that determine achievement will help us create more systems and structures to support more women in their quest to succeed. As our women succeed, our children, communities, and countries succeed. Our countries will succeed and thrive. Our countries will succeed and thrive as our people prosper. African countries must be associated with success.

As she meanderingly tells her story in *Fearless*, one can't help but feel the tenacity that continues to propel her – even in the moments when she clearly doubts herself. The girl from the slums who rose to build a successful senior executive career in the unlikely field of telecommunications bolstered by her degree in Engineering. Let that sink in. As it sinks in, picture the contrast that is Jane Egerton-Idehen! A meeting of two worlds that could not be more different.

As you read and feel drawn in by this story, have a pen and notebook handy. Take notes and write the lessons learnt. Jane lives to see the next woman do better.

Doing better was exactly her approach when she interviewed me for her platform, 'Women and Career.' It was a year or two after our first meeting and we ended up spending over an hour discussing what it takes to build a successful career. As women we not only need mentoring and coaching from other women; we should also be open to mentoring, coaching, and sponsorship of male allies who are further along in their careers. This is especially true for us women who have chosen to work in what are still male-dominated fields. Women need mentoring and sponsorship that are above board every step of the way.

Women do not have to compromise their values to succeed. Values must remain firm and if our values mean a slightly longer-winded path to success, then so be it.

It is my deepest hope that as young people in particular read this book, the young women will draw strength from Jane's example and the young men will commit to being allies that support the women around them in their journeys.

Thank you Jane for authentically allowing us into your world to learn from you, to seek out joy, and grow in tenacity to realise our dreams!

Lucy Quist
Author, ***The Bold New Normal***

Introduction

What happens when a girl from the slums dares to dream? She bags an engineering degree and an executive education from Harvard Business School, she becomes a leader in the telecommunications industry, and she mentors other girls and women to do the same.

In Be *Fearless: Give Yourself Permission to Be You,* Jane Egerton-Idehen draws from her more than 15 years of experience as a telecommunication executive in West Africa to help women build lasting careers, especially in the male-dominated STEM industries. Rising from the slums of Ajegunle in Lagos, Nigeria, to brokering million-dollar deals for global telecoms giants, hers is a story of hope, of challenging traditional gender roles, and of embracing who you are. This is a book about women for women, as well as the men who love, nurture, support, and work with them at home and in the office.

The *Women Matter Africa* report, by McKinsey & Company, notes that in Africa, there is an 18-percent "leakage" of women in senior management positions, compared with nonmanagement positions. In STEM industries, the leakage may well be more. For many females in the workplace today, the challenge is no longer access but equality—the quest to receive equal treatment when it comes to opportunities, promotions, hiring, pay increases, and line management positions.

Writing with the girl or woman who dreams of more in mind, Jane is a daughter, sister, friend, telecoms executive, wife, mother, mentor, coach—and dreamer. In *Fearless*, she explores and demystifies the cultural expectations, biases, and seemingly impossible hurdles that women must confront to turn their wishful thinking and dreams into career successes. Peppered with candid anecdotes, the book discusses her less-privileged background, education, career journey, marriage, motherhood, mentoring, and passions in the easy style that she uses to engage audiences during her speaking tours.

Nigeria has one of the largest youth populations in the world, with females making up half that population. Understanding the challenges faced by this demographic group is key to unleashing the potential power of the workforce. Therefore, if you are a father, mother, grandparent, uncle, aunt, brother, sister, teacher, colleague, friend, or role model, this book is for you too. Even if it might make you uncomfortable, it is time to give the women around you permission to be who they are.

CHAPTER 1

The Caged Bird

I attended a strict secondary school with boarding facilities, where school life was governed by a million rules that had to be obeyed—or else! We observed set times for lunch, dinner, classes, study preparation, and sleep. I felt like a caged bird.

Once I began my university education, I felt like that caged bird that had been set free. I was an adult, and I could make all the decisions about how I spent my time. Eager to exploit my independence, I determined to change the world, and I projected in my voice and demeanor all the confidence that my 18-year-old self could muster.

I met Peace at the University of Nigeria, Nsukka (UNN), when I was a first-year undergraduate studying industrial chemistry. Peace was a senior, studying mechanical engineering. His smile exposed a gap between two of his upper front teeth, which distinguished him from the other boys. He was nicely built, dark, with very attractive features. One day, he stopped me on my way to lunch at one of the campus canteens that I frequented with my good friend, Chinwe. Not long after our initial meeting, Peace and I began to take long walks around campus together.

UNN is located in the high plains of the Udi Hills in Enugu State, in southeastern Nigeria. It was the first indigenous Nigerian university, founded in 1955 by Nnamdi Azikiwe, who would later be Nigeria's first president. I relished the clean, crisp air in serene Nsukka, because I had grown up in Lagos, Nigeria's equivalent of New York

City. The air in Lagos was polluted, heavy with fumes and particulate matter from the exhaust pipes of countless vehicles as well as industrial emissions. In Nsukka, by contrast, I would sometimes taste tiny particles released into the air by the dry red soil, which surrounded the trees and plants that beautified our campus. During the last few months of the year, when I met Peace, we usually experienced humid days and cold nights.

When I was on campus, I typically wore flat shoes, flannel shirts or bland blouses, and plain straight skirts, giving the general impression of a tomboy. In response to anyone who dared to comment on my looks, I simply explained that I valued my intelligence more than a fashionable appearance. Chinwe, unlike me, had been groomed by her mother to be a very chic and stylish lady. She often talked me through matching colours, prints, and fabrics. But my first and only attempt at putting my look together was making sure that the colours of my outfits were uniform. At some point, everything in my wardrobe was mostly blue—even my umbrella—because it made my life easier.

I avoided wearing makeup on campus, and I kept my thick, kinky hair short. I sometimes relaxed my hair, chemically altering its texture, but it refused to stay down and flat in a way that signified sophistication. I considered myself to be my father's daughter—meaning that I did not bother with vanity. In reality, though, money was tight, and I did not have enough for what I considered superficial extras. It was simply cheaper to ignore my looks.

Peace, on the other hand, was always very well groomed, and he gave a lot of attention to his appearance. He shaved every day and wore aftershave and cologne, which I thought was very vain. He loved to wear faded jeans and light-coloured cotton shirts. He usually unbuttoned the top of his shirt to reveal about an inch of the white round-neck t-shirt that he wore beneath. He completed his ensemble with sandals or loafers. He was not one for suits and formalwear.

Falling in Love

During our evening walks, Peace and I discussed—and sometimes argued over—topics that intrigued us. We debated issues surrounding scientific inventions and inventors, global politics, race, pop culture, and culture in general. I guess he enjoyed the company of a practical and determined young lady willing to voice her opinions and question the status quo. I loved the fact that I could share my thoughts and challenge some of his opinions with impunity. Late in the evening, after we finished studying, we continued our debates as he walked me back to my room. If we couldn't agree, we called a truce and continued the debate at our next meeting. In the interim, I carried out research, gathering more information to buttress my points. I anticipated our next meeting with pleasure, and I secretly enjoyed the fact that my arguments were having an impact on him. I was glad that he was interested in my brains, not my looks. I have always been attracted to intellectual men, and Peace listened to me and took my opinions seriously. I felt as though he really saw me for who I was.

I once tried to make a case for Peace to stop smoking, trying to persuade him on health grounds. I believed that his smoking had become a disgusting sport. He competed with his roommates to see who had the largest collection of cigarette stubs, which they housed in jars. I decided to catch his attention by flipping the script, asking, "How would you feel if I smoked?" Shocked, he replied that he would probably be worried for me. Culturally in Nigeria at that time, it was more acceptable for men to smoke than women. Smoking was perceived as cool for men. However, women who smoked cigarettes were seen as wayward. To me, the adverse health effects on both genders were the same.

Peace challenged my intellect when we argued. I can clearly recall one debate we had about the factors that drive the different genders in relationships. The common school of thought then was that women were attracted to a man's physical attributes, personality, and material possessions. I insisted that this generalization was skewed and that there were other things that women looked for in men. We were walking on the hilly dirt road that ran from the male hostel to the canteen area—just two students unaware of others who strolled or scurried past, all of us creating circles of dust as our footwear slapped the ground. Then Peace stopped and looked at me directly. He asked, "Would you marry a one-armed man or a Muslim?" He knew that I was a Christian and that, traditionally, Muslims and Christians hardly marry. I nodded in the affirmative, saying, "If he meets the values that are important to me, and we have chemistry."

We often discussed patriarchy and male privilege. One particular discussion took place in my hostel room, and all four of my roommates got involved. Peace stated that beyond a certain age, single women with powerful careers would struggle to find a male partner. He cited Oprah Winfrey as an example. I argued otherwise, because I opposed some of the unrealistic assumptions made about women in marriage. For example, I asked if marriage was compulsory. Peace teased me by saying, "Be careful, girl, that you don't become one of those powerful ladies who is not married at thirty and then becomes desperate." We always argued from opposite sides, but we truly enjoyed each other's company.

Later that year, Peace and I started dating. I was 19 years old. I broke my rule of not dating while I was a student. But I had I fallen in love hard, and so had he. I wrote poems about him, discovering my latent creativity brought about by love. For most of the time while we dated, I was studying engineering at UNN, having changed my major from industrial chemistry in my second year. Meanwhile, he graduated and began working as an engineer for an oil company. So, we began living apart. It seemed as if we wrote letters to each other every day. I read and reread his letters for days and weeks, and he did the same with mine.

Peace was very generous with me, frequently sending me a living allowance. I knew that he had major responsibilities. His job had taken him to a new city. He had to get an apartment and a car, and he had younger siblings to support. Yet, he still cared about my financial state. I was reluctant to invite people to my home because we lived in the slums, and I was ashamed of my living conditions. However, Peace and I shared such openness and trust that I allowed myself to be vulnerable, and he visited me at home.

I remember that immediately after he returned from his first business trip to Europe, he made the eight-hour road trip to Nsukka to see me at school. He barely stopped to drop his bags at home. I savoured our reunion, listening to stories about his European trip. With him, I felt special, loved, and desired. He was a blessing during my years at the university.

Will You Marry Me?

Peace was attentive and charming. His good looks and his good job made most young women consider him a great catch. In the course of our relationship, we both agreed to get married. The plan was to do this after I graduated and got a job.

However, in the fourth year of our relationship, in 2000, I began to feel like I was losing my voice, while he became more confident, almost to the point of arrogance. I recall one altercation at his home during one of the weekends that I visited him. I wanted to cook for us, and I asked him to drive me to the market. Although he had no other plans for the day, he was reluctant to take me. He recommended that I take the public transport. Something about that response made me feel very vulnerable. I needed his presence, and I wanted him to go with me. I was a visitor in town, and I didn't know my way around. That added to my discomfort because I was also feeling a little guilty about being there without the knowledge of my parents. They were not aware that I had left school for the weekend to spend time with Peace. So now I imagined myself being married to him, being heavily pregnant, stranded while shopping, and calling him to come pick me up. I imagined that he would insist that I use public transportation because picking me up was inconvenient for him.

Doubts surfaced in my mind. Had we lost that spark, that desire to sacrifice and go the extra mile for each other? Why was I losing the ability to speak up about my discomfort? Were we letting cultural stereotypes steal what we had—with the husband being the lord and master of the home, while his domesticated wife assumes the invisible role of taking care of the family and shelving her own dreams? Our dynamics and reality as a couple started to tilt toward the direction that we detested.

A couple of months after I graduated, I landed my first job as an intern at a telecommunication company in Lagos. I was twenty-five, and Peace had just turned thirty. He had long wanted to get married at thirty and had worked to achieve that goal. My parents refused to bless our engagement because Peace and I hailed from different tribes. At some point, he insisted that it was my role to convince my parents. I did not know how to do that. In many ways, I was still dependent on them. I felt that only time could convince them, but he didn't want to wait. He wanted me to elope with him. I loved him, but I was not ready for that. Although I felt obligated to marry Peace, considering how kind and supportive he had been during my university days, and although I disagreed with my parents' decision, something did not add up for me.

Between the 1960s and early 2000s, research revealed a pronounced trend toward delayed marriage in much of the world. In the United States, for example, the median age at marriage had reached 27 for men and 25 for women by 2004. It had gone up from 23 for men and 20 for women during 1950 -1960 (U.S. Census Bureau, 2004). Most importantly, the reasons for these later ages at marriage include changing male and female employment opportunities (Fitch and Ruggles, 2000), the growth of cohabitation as a living arrangement, and the emerging view of marriage as a transition to be postponed until financial security has been attained (Cherlin, 2004). The U.S. median age of marriage is old for women in the African context.

In my case, I delayed marriage due to a mixture of factors, prominent among them being the desire to attain my own financial security. All my life, I had been dependent on someone else for financial support. The fact that I was financially dependent on Peace had exacerbated the other issues we faced. When I obtained a job, my newfound financial independence brought a subtle confidence to question my motives for wanting to get married at that stage in my life. In addition, I had serious financial obligations to meet at home. My sister and I were responsible for paying the school fees of our two young brothers. At that time in Nigeria, the government did not provide free education or welfare benefits. Our parents could not afford to pay their fees, and I suspect that this need for my financial help contributed to my parents' rejection of Peace's marriage proposal to me.

Numerous studies show that individuals who marry at young ages tend to be at high risk of marital dissolution.[1] I would add that most young women in patriarchal cultures, such as in West Africa, are not financially independent. They lack the authority to navigate the complexities involved in managing the various stakeholders required in a union such as marriage (including parents, in-laws, extended family, and the community). These women are yet to evolve fully into their own. I think that for most young women in these cultures, there is a correlation between financial independence and assertiveness in a relationship. Financial independence tipped the balance in my relationship, positioning me to follow my dreams and question if my ambition was embraced and supported by my partner—not just in words but also in actions.

[1] (Bumpass *et al.*, 1991; Castro-Martin and Bumpass, 1989; Lehrer 1996; Teachman, 2002)

Sacrifices

In 2002, I was working with a team of engineers overseeing an earth, or ground, station (for communicating with satellites). It was a demanding job, and we ran a duty schedule with everyone on the roster. I was not exempted from the night shift. Because I was the only female on the team, I would have seen such an exemption as biased. I was there to work and learn, like everyone else, irrespective of gender or shift time. However, Peace insinuated that after we got married, I should take a teaching job close to our home, or work for a company with less burdensome hours. He reasoned that it would be less demanding and less stressful for me and give me more time for our family. "Less demanding and less stressful" were the wrong words for him to use because they were not the criteria that I used to choose a place to work and to develop my career.

Thus, I found myself feeling like a caged bird again, imprisoned by the expectations of my role as a wife. But because I felt obligated to Peace by the years invested in our relationship, I could not set myself free. Within the patriarchal paradigm of Nigeria, the child-bearing and child-rearing responsibilities are considered the main goals in a woman's life. These goals do not require any special investment or capacity-building. [2] This cultural norm adds an unfair expectation on the female gender to inherently sacrifice everything for the ultimate goal of raising children.

As I previously mentioned, I felt like I was losing my voice. I did not talk about my concerns, so Peace was oblivious to them. In my quiet moments, I nursed my doubts alone. Since then, I have asked myself several times why I never fought to speak up. Why didn't I voice my convictions about what the proper power balance in the relationship should be? Why didn't Peace notice that the formerly outspoken girl seemed to be withholding this side of herself?

---

[2] (Nainar, 2013)

The insidious nature of patriarchy creates victims in both males and females. Even good men who view themselves as feminists make choices that show their unconscious biases. In the end, we are all victims of the prevailing system. As Tony Porter, an author, educator, and activist working to advance social justice, says, "My liberation as a man is tied to your liberation as a woman." As long as we live in a patriarchal society, the majority of men will not be truly free.

During this tough time in our relationship, Peace insisted that the onus was on the girlfriend to visit her boyfriend. I was guilt-ridden. I wanted to make up for the long trips he had made to Nsukka to visit me. So, once a month, I made a round trip between Lagos and Benin by road to spend a couple of hours with him—four hours from Lagos to Benin and then another four hours from Benin back to Lagos. I fooled my parents into believing that I was at work, and only my sister knew the truth. I could not let my mother know that I was spending the night with Peace in Benin. (Sorry, mum, if you are reading this.)

Despite my efforts and sacrifices, the issues between Peace and me were not getting resolved, and I continued to struggle to meet his expectations. He suddenly found fault with matters that I thought were unimportant, like my wardrobe. At one point, I declared, "Okay, from now on, I will wear jeans and t-shirts, if that makes you happy!" And I made the change that he recommended.

My questions grew and intensified. Was this the life and career I wanted? What happened to my dreams about changing the world through my engineering career? What about the discussions we had during school? We were both engineers, so why should he work as an engineer while I worked as a teacher?

In August 2002, during the sixth year of our relationship, we broke up. The first thing I did after the breakup was to submit my application for the master's degree program in engineering at Massachusetts Institute of Technology (MIT) in the United States. I had harboured a dream about attending MIT since my first year at university. Nothing could stop me now, and I wanted to get away from the disappointment of a broken heart. I made a pact with myself to not date anyone for one year, so I could heal and be clear about what I wanted in a male partner and what I expected in a marriage.

In some ways, Peace turned out to be right. At age thirty, I was unmarried—but I was not desperate. By then, I understood the power of being intentional in my actions. Did I feel free? The thought did not cross my mind much then. I suspect that I saw myself as an injured bird perching at the doorway of my open cage. I was clear about flight directions, but I was recuperating, seeking the energy to fly.

CHAPTER 2

I Have a Dream (I)

My earliest childhood memories are of time spent in the Tunkanrimu area of Ajegunle, a slum located close to two of the busiest ports in Nigeria, Tincan Island and Lagos Port Complex. There were no parking spaces for cars, and the houses resembled pieces of a giant jigsaw puzzle because they were built in a haphazard manner. We lived at the bottom of a slope. I remember looking up the hill, scanning the faces of women as they walked down, searching for my mum in the crowd. I wonder why I panicked and worried about her making it back home. Could it be because my mum was at the core of all the activities in our home? She was the voice and conductor of our family orchestra at the bungalow we called home.

Houses in our part of town were mostly bungalows, with a long corridor inside and adjacent rooms on either side of the corridor. Hence, such homes were nicknamed "face-me-I-face-you." Usually, individuals or families rented the rooms, and they left their doors open to aid ventilation, with a flimsy curtain hanging across the doorway. This meant that you could see all that happened in your neighbour's world.

Our house stood within a series of narrow lanes several right turns off of the main motorable road. Our bungalow was slightly different than the others. It consisted of apartments with a main entrance that faced the road. Each apartment had two or three rooms. On any given late afternoon, an individual walking by would observe sparsely clad children playing, peddlers and hawkers advertising their wares, and parents sitting by the buildings, discussing or observing the flow of human traffic. It was the bustle and chaos of common people living and loving life.

We had some rather interesting neighbours. I very much remember a family from the northern part of Nigeria, people who hailed from the Hausa tribe. I was good friends with one of the daughters. who was about my age. Unfortunately, I think she was betrothed to her future husband when she was only six years old, so she had no plans for school. But I admired her long, plaited hair. My dad required me to keep my hair short because he believed that growing long hair was a distraction for girls. I suspect that he did not want us looking too attractive or risk being derailed by vain ideas of external beauty. This girl's hair looked beautiful but smelled badly because she did not wash it for months at a time. However, hair was the least of our worries as little girls.

Right next to the Hausa family lived a mean and noisy neighbour. He got into a fight with my mum when she was pregnant with my youngest brother, Chidi. He and certain other neighbours would sometimes yell over little things, such as dropping litter in front of the house, not sweeping the front of your veranda, or looking at them in a perceived "evil" manner. Life in the "jungle" (that was how we referred to Ajegunle) could be crazy like that. During the altercation with my mum, someone called the police, and we had to stay home with a relative who took care of us while my mum was at the police station. Looking back, I believe that the aggression that people displayed then was their way of pouring out their frustrations on others—whomever happened to be closest.

My Love for Reading

Our veranda had a door that led to our sitting room. We had a couple of seats and a TV encased in a wooden box. My dad entertained visitors, and the family ate meals, watched television, and enjoyed each other's company here. I remember a remarkable photo taken in this room, in which my mum was eating a piece of *eba* (a local dish made from cassava and eaten with soup) while the entire family gathered around her smiling. My sister, Nneka, carried Chidi, the youngest child, on her hips. A wooden table stood at the centre of the room, and it served as our dining table. My dad was keen to promote unity in the family, and he thought food was a symbolic way to do that, so we all ate together at the table. Our meals were not eaten separately, as I frequently observed in the homes of my friends.

At the end of the room, in the left-hand corner, was a door that opened into the bedroom. There was one bed for dad and another one for mum. The kids slept with either parent. All our belongings were kept in this room. We had a blue refrigerator, which faced the door. It was considered a luxury item, hence its location in the bedroom.

My dad's bookshelf was located at the right-hand side of the bedroom. He was a very private man who spent his spare time watching the news or reading. Although he had attended neither secondary school nor college, he sought knowledge like it was gold. My love for books is derived from him, and I acquired my reading habits from watching him. His bookshelf was filled with spiritual books, including publications on oriental religions and conspiracies surrounding Christianity, as well as books on baking and selections from classic literature. My first exposure to *Romeo and Juliet*, *Jane Eyre*, and Chinua Achebe's *Things Fall Apart* was from my dad's library.

According to UNICEF, without skills for lifelong learning, children face greater barriers to their earning potential and their employment later in life. They are more likely to suffer adverse health outcomes and less likely to participate in the decisions that affect them—threatening their ability to build a better future for themselves and their communities.[3] I couldn't agree more. Reading is a skill that aids learning—and life.

Did the seeds of my inner voice emanate from those books? They triggered my imagination and created a world beyond my immediate environment—a world in which I could dream and aspire to explore.

Education is the Key to Freedom

My father was the secretary of a director at an oil company. He was an excellent typist, and he was very good at shorthand (a method of taking notes)—key skills for such positions at that time. Interestingly enough, my mother possessed those skills as well, and during the early years of their marriage, they both worked. As the family story went, my mother had to give up her career when she came home one day to find my older sister, Nneka, eating sand while playing.

[3] (UNICEF, 2019a)

Apparently, my dad expressed concerns, saying that he wanted my mum to stay home and take care of the kids.

I have since come to realize the amazing sacrifice that my mother made, how she repeatedly gave up her own dreams to ensure that our dreams as a family came true. The impact of the decision to have kids for working families is less intrusive on the careers of men than women, and I discuss this in more detail in chapter 6.

My dad's "side hustle" was a bakery, which he originally owned with a friend who shared the same faith as him. My dad was not a Christian, and he was quick to let everyone know that. He toyed with several religions, from Mormonism to Seventh-day Adventist, before settling on Mumihie (pronounced *mom-mi-hay*). That is an oriental blend of religions started by a Nigerian doctor who had spent a long time in Far-East Asia studying various religions.

While my dad went to work at the oil company, my mum ran the bakery. The business benefitted from the skills of my energetic mum. I recall mornings when she fussed over dad, offering him tea before he caught the staff bus to work. She dressed us up early to catch the school bus by 6:00 a.m. Then she was off to the bakery to sell freshly baked bread to resellers. She always had support from cousins and other relatives who stayed with us. Our house always smelled of freshly baked bread, which we had in bountiful supply. Our relatives joked that we could brush our teeth with bread instead of water. I grew up loving and eating so much bread that I still struggle with the current trend of avoiding bread made from wheat, and the perceived unhealthy nature of white flour.

You could tell we were the "middle class" of the slums because we lived in more than one room and attended a private school. In the slums, most children attended public schools or no school at all. But my parents strongly believed in education. They told us that it would be our one ticket out of poverty, and they would do their very best to give us a good education.

The fourth of the seventeen United Nations Sustainable Development Goals (SDGs) is quality education. According to the UN, obtaining a quality education is the foundation to creating sustainable development. In addition to improving quality of life, access to inclusive education can help equip local officials with the tools required to develop innovative solutions to the world's greatest problems.[4]

Self-Awareness

My elementary school was called Hope Children Nursery and Primary School. I must have been about seven and in primary two when I realized that my thoughts were private. Our teacher had asked the entire class to be quiet and read a book. As she walked around the class, she commended me for "doing a good job." I was shocked because I was simply staring at the book in front of me while I was daydreaming. I was surprised that she had no clue as to what I was really doing, and I was fascinated that she was not aware of the internal dialogue I was having about the incident. I smile even as I write this, because it was something I discovered myself, no one taught me. This was self-awareness!

The thoughts in my head evolved into dreams of who I wanted to be. I had early dreams of being an entertainer. The glitz and glamor of the variety TV shows of the 1980s, like *Donny & Marie*, must have caught my attention. I spent some days putting on shows for my imaginary audience. These places in my head became a zone of comfort in which to escape when things became tough later on in life. They were places where I could go and create the world that I wanted. For example, I sometimes saw myself in a white pantsuit walking up the steps of a magnificent and large office building, holding my executive briefcase, exuding confidence, and smiling. Other times, I just dreamt of having my own typewriters.

---

[4] (United Nations, 2019c).

These images never left me. Now, I have learned how to not only create the images in my head, but also to bring them to life.

Life is Full of Surprises

In 1987, I discovered that I did not make the required grades in the common entrance examination to be admitted to a federal-government-owned secondary school. I was eleven years old. My parents had dreamt about this for all of us as far back as I could remember. Somewhere along the line, we bought into their dream. I know at that point in my life, I wanted to attend one of those schools. My sister had taken the exam twice and failed, so she had to attend one of the crowded state-government schools in the area. I didn't want to have to do that. That Christmas, I fell seriously ill with malaria, and my mother thought it was because of the sad news.

Early the next year, I got into an overcrowded public school in my area called Trinity Secondary School. I suspect that my parents had pushed us through private primary schools to better our chances of getting into the federal government colleges, or "unity schools," as they were called. They were good schools that were subsidized by the federal government, and they had affordable fees for families that could not pay for private secondary schools. However, a quota system and the federal principle were policies used in the admission process. Nigeria is a multiethnic federation of thirty-six states, and both policies were aimed at ensuring that students from educationally disadvantaged states stood a chance at acquiring quality education. Those students were admitted into the colleges even if they had low grades. We hailed from the parts of the country with good educational standards. Therefore, admission was highly competitive, and a student needed exceptional grades to gain entry into the colleges.

I was shocked at the conditions in my new school. The infrastructure was alarming, even for the slums. For weeks, I could not get over it. Classes were rowdy and noisy. Some teachers did not bother to show up, and students turned those classes into whatever kind of environment they wanted.

In some regions, most notably in sub-Saharan Africa, the lack of trained teachers and the poor conditions of the schools are jeopardizing the goal of quality education for all. Sub-Saharan Africa has the lowest percentage of trained teachers in all three levels of schooling: 44 percent in pre-primary, 74 percent in primary, and 55 percent in secondary education.[5]

Business leaders around the world have recognized education as one of the most urgent sustainability challenges. However, business investments in education have often been small, short-term, uncoordinated, and unequally distributed. Increasing smart investment in education over the longer term is necessary. Investment in education expands business opportunities, creating new markets and customer bases. It also results in a more skilled workforce, increasing productivity and driving business growth. A more educated and skilled workforce leads to better wages and more disposable income for consumer spending.[6]

English is the official language of Nigeria. In addition, Yoruba, Igbo, and Hausa are widely spoken, with Yoruba spoken in the southwestern part of the country. I vaguely recall our Yoruba language teacher. She unapologetically spoke Yoruba in her class, with no trace of English. She claimed that this practice would improve our fluency in Yoruba. I panicked, because although I had lived in

[5] (United Nations, 2017).
[6] (United Nations, 2019a).

Lagos all my life, I could barely speak Yoruba. My postcolonial parents hoped to improve our fluency of English by banning us from speaking vernacular and local, traditional languages. They may have also perceived our mastery of English as a status symbol. I know that my dad wanted his kids to have mastery of the English language, so even our ethnic language, Igbo, was not deliberately taught at home I never could achieve fluency in yet another language.

As I walked home from school, I was alarmed by the waywardness of some of the students. Near the school were a couple shops selling car parts that were managed by my fellow Igbos. The young male apprentices in these shops would often make advances toward the secondary school girls. My new school was full of teenagers with raging hormones who lacked adult supervision. These kinds of children are vulnerable, especially the girls. As noted by UNICEF, adolescence represents a transition from childhood to physical and psychological maturity, and adolescent girls are particularly vulnerable because they face the risks of premature pregnancy and childbirth.[7]

Some students never showed up to school, or they came to classes only when they felt like it. Life at Trinity Secondary School was much different from the order and structure of my primary school. I stuck to friends that I knew from primary school, other girls like me, whose parents could not afford private education and who did not make it to the federal government colleges. My friends and I studied together, we exchanged notes, and we always attended classes. We spent our spare time inspiring one another with stories of people who had gone through this troubled school system and still made it to university. I was searching for normalcy, and I wanted to make something positive out of the situation.

1988 was the year in which my life turned around. I believe that God decided to change my path and my destiny at that time.

[7] (UNICEF, 2019b).

I could never have influenced any of the events that happened, and they have since formed one of the anchor stories that I run to whenever I'm at a crossroads and cannot find a path to my desired goals. I have learned that sometimes in life, God has a way of moving obstacles, and all we have to do is relax and walk along the path that is opened for us.

About six weeks into my mini hell at school, I came home to see my parents looking excited. They wanted me to read the contents of an envelope that had just come in the mail for me. As usual, they had read it first. The envelope was brown, bulging with the multiple papers it contained. Some of the documents had fabric samples pinned to them. I would later discover they were sample fabrics for the school uniform. Once they told me what it was about, I could not hold back my joy. I was so happy! And as I read through the papers, I made plans on how to respond.

I had just been admitted into one of the federal government colleges. It was a boarding school for girls in eastern Nigeria—the Federal Government Girls' College in Owerri, Imo State. I did not recall choosing this college, which was relatively far from my home. My parents and I had chosen college options closer to where we lived in the southwest. But at that moment, no one cared. My mother calculated that she could quickly sell my dad's now rundown bakery to raise funds, and my parents considered travel dates to visit the college. Interestingly, classes had actually started in January, but we had only just received the admission letter in early February.

I remember going to the bedroom that all six of us (dad, mum, and my three siblings) shared and jumping on my dad's bed. It was the best bouncing-castle ride ever and the purest form of joy that I had experienced up to that time. It is an ecstatic memory that has never left me, carefully tucked away and saved for those special moments when I need to put a smile on my face or motivate myself. I guess it is one reason that, today, I find it hard to stop my kids from bouncing on their beds. This story is symbolic for me because it marked the start of my journey into a life filled with wonder. I dream big because my dreams somehow find a way of coming to life.

Her Mother's Daughter

Before I tell you about my college years and the rest of my journey, I'd like to share a little more about my life at home during my time in secondary school. Although the school was unpleasant, I was able to find comfort at home. My heart always skipped a beat whenever I heard the call for dinner, which was usually a bell ringing to the tune of "Girls Come and Eat." Considering my family's financial situation, I would feel privileged. I could not believe that we ate three square meals a day!

You see, my dad had resigned from his job with the oil company in 1983 to run the family bakery business with my mum and his friend. But the partnership with his friend turned sour, and they found themselves battling in court. This was partly the result of the government banning the importation of many goods in 1984. Flour, a key ingredient for baking bread, was one of these banned goods. Nigeria is a massive market for wheat consumption, but low local production means it is heavily dependent on imported wheat supplies. This ban triggered a huge scarcity of wheat flour. My dad tried to use alternatives to make the bread, but it never turned out well. He resorted to selling his assets and trying to retrieve bad loans that he had given in the past, while he searched for other business opportunities.

It eventually became a struggle to afford just two meals a day at home. My mum bought beef bones from the market to make broth for soup. She joked that she told the butcher the bones were for her dogs. She was a die-hard survivor, always looking for creative ways to make ends meet. She was also a realistic optimist, and she believed that "one day, it [the struggles] shall be over." That was her often-repeated phrase. Later in life, I drew from her strength—her attitude of never giving up, kicking the door open when faced with opposition, and refusing to walk away from it all, either in my marriage or my career.

Many students from middle-class Nigeria told tales about their homes that intrigued me during these challenging years. Don't get me wrong, we had girls from all kinds of backgrounds—including some whose financial situations were worse than mine. But I guess it was sometimes all a bit too much for this poor but smart kid. I felt like a drifter trying to find my place in a melting pot of students.

The Sound of Rain

Wangari Marthai (a renowned Kenyan social, environmental, and political activist, as well as the first African woman to win a Nobel Prize) said, "There are opportunities even in the most difficult moments." I have some sad emotional triggers when it rains, stemming from difficult moments in my childhood. The pitter-patter of rain reminds me of the lonely and uncomfortable feeling of sleeping on cold, damp metal springs.

During my preteen and teenage years, I often wet my bed. While at home, this did not deeply concern me. My mum kept an eye on my water intake during the evenings to ensure that I drank fewer fluids, and she sometimes woke me up at night to make me use the bathroom. When I got to boarding school, however, I had to manage the situation myself. It was a baptism into independence by fire. On days when I wet my bed, I woke up filled with guilt, self-loathing, and sadness. I would take my mattress outside and wash the affected areas, then leave it to dry in the sun. During the first year at boarding school, I slept on the top bunk, and some nights, urine dripped on my bunkmate beneath.

You can imagine how badly bedwetting affected my self-esteem. I deliberately kept a very small friendship circle. I lacked confidence. I was sometimes victimized by my peers, who would send me on pointless errands just to make fun of me. I wished it would end!

On nights when I wet my bed, I sometimes slept with a blanket spread over the wet spots. This situation was extremely embarrassing for me, and I felt that it was also unfair to my roommates, who had to bear with the stench of my damp and dirty mattress. Nevertheless, this experience tested my problem-solving skills. I took charge of the situation. I started to carefully monitor my water intake. I sometimes buddied up with a friend, who woke me up at night when she was going to relieve herself. I even made a pact with God, promising that if He solved this embarrassing problem, I was all His. I learned that life skills for the future come through several experiences, and not all of them are enjoyable.

Angels Along the Way

Visiting and end-of-term days were especially tough in secondary school. The first Sunday of the month was designated as visiting day. Guardians, parents, or other relatives were allowed to visit the school and check on their loved ones. The hostels, where the students lived, bustled with activity as students prepared to hear over the loudspeaker that they had visitors. We dressed in white sleeveless blouses with a bow and blue skirts. Parents and guardians gathered at the school stadium, sitting in their cars or in the bleachers to meet the students. The school had a stadium for sports but which also doubled as a venue for visiting parents. Eventually, smiling students poured back into the hostels with food and provisions, chatting about the visits.

On some visiting days, my Uncle Edmund, who was actually an older cousin, came around with a loaf of bread and a large bottle of soda. Edmund was a taxi driver who lived in Okigwe, a couple of kilometers from the school. I later found out that he had loaned my dad part of my initial school fees. My uncle remains a selfless man with a big heart, an angel to me. He has been married for over thirty years but has no offspring. Later, during my university days and early in my career, I would send Uncle Edmund small gifts and letters, which I signed as "Your daughter, Nkechi." (Nkechi is my Igbo name.) These days, I try to live up to that role because even angels need love.

I am eternally grateful to Uncle Edmund for showing up whenever he could on visiting days. I guess it made me feel loved to hear my name over the loudspeaker, "Nkechi Amadi, come over to the stadium, someone is here to see you."

For some of us whose parents or guardians lived in other states, they would visit us maybe once a term. For others, it was a wish and dream that rarely or never happened.

And I Found Jane

My awakening and drive to improve my academics came from the combination of a serendipitous moment and a couple of other events. I spent my mid-term breaks at school, because going back home to the city for a one-week break was a luxury. My options were to spend my break in the village (the rural area where my extended family lived) or with my Uncle Edmund in Okigwe. I spent this one particular mid-term at school.

Mid-terms were fun, because our rigid school routines were absent. We ate, slept, played games, bantered, and recalled stories from home, such as movies we had watched. My family did not have a VCR at home (at a time when most people watched movies on VCRs), so I had no movie stories to share. I was very self-conscious of the fact that I came from a slum in Ajegunle. I learned to compartmentalize the personal information that I shared with others. During such conversations, I knew the exit points, and I became skilled at deflecting attention from myself while enjoying the moment. I heard some of the movie reviews so many times that today, if you ask me if I have seen any of those movies, I feel like I could answer, "yes."

During that term, we had attended preparatory classes (prep) after siesta to do homework and read ahead of the next day's classes. But at mid-term, the rules about what we did during prep were slack.

I was so bored one day, with nothing much to do, that I started to write what I was reading on the classroom blackboard. I was studying Chemistry. Then I explained my understanding of the chemistry topic to my imaginary audience. After a couple of sessions, I noticed that I derived pleasure from being a pseudo-teacher. Today, as I write about this, I get warm feelings because it brings back the sense of fulfillment that I derived from this act. I guess that was my first exposure to one of my strengths: the ability to break down complex topics and present them in a simple manner that is also entertaining.

When school resumed, I realized that I could answer questions in chemistry class that most other students could not answer. I had read so much of the chemistry textbook that was used by the school that I could cite the exact pages from the book that buttressed my points. I took an interest in other girls who did the same. I noticed that they were paying to take extra classes during prep, as some of them were preparing to take the final exams early. I yearned for an opportunity to join them. I saved up some money from wherever I could and invested it in this venture. I did not tell my parents about it. In hindsight, I see that I was driven by my innate tendency to be competitive.

The educational venture paid off. In my sixth year, I earned six As and two Cs in the final external exams. I made A1—the highest possible grade—in physics, chemistry, mathematics, and advanced math. Later in life, during my career (when I was being referred to as Jane rather than Nkechi), I displayed advanced versions of the skills and traits that I had discovered during this phase of my life. They proved to be crucial in progressing my career.

No Place for Dreams?

While growing up in Ajegunle, on a cordoned-off portion of swampy land, two small structures built with wooden planks sat atop stilts. Those were how some toilets were built. They were constructed such that when adults went about their business, their waste dropped directly into buckets positioned underneath in the swamp. Because these outdoor toilets were raised on stilts and separated from the living area, everyone thought the arrangement was okay. The distance from the living area to the toilets was about fifty metres, accessible across a wooden ramp. Kids usually just found a dry spot on the wooden walkway to do their business. The kids needed no privacy, as they enjoyed the beautiful view of birds flying in the sky above. The kids played in the grassy field, which was just ten metres from the toilet area.

That was how the toilets of most of our neighbours were built—on stilts over a swamp. Our bungalow, however, had an extension at the back, which served as our toilet, and a bucket was used to collect the waste. Masked men wearing boots came routinely to collect the buckets when they were full, and they emptied them into a truck that took the waste for disposal. The waste product was similar to the "night soil" collected by men in early Victorian times before the advent of plumbing or sewage systems.

This was an unhygienic and chaotic environment. Yet, I would sit there and look up at the sky and dream about all the things that life could bring me. I believe that anyone, anywhere, under any circumstances can and should dream.

CHAPTER 3

I Have a Dream (II)

Somewhere along the way, I decided to study engineering. I believe that God or the universe somehow intervened to support me in that pursuit. I once eavesdropped on a conversation between my mum and her godmother (an older friend who acted as her marriage sponsor). The lady said that her son was studying engineering, and she added that the subject was so difficult that many students were failing. I was so intrigued by what I heard that I wanted to study engineering. I have always been attracted to a challenge. Tell me something is difficult and can't be done, and you have my attention. I am still learning to apply this self-knowledge and use it as a springboard to push boundaries in my life.

In boarding school, we were advised to choose our subjects according to what we wanted to study in university. My parents wanted me to study medicine, but I did not want to do that. After our disagreement on the matter, I did not bring it up again with them. This offered a glimpse into how I would deal with conflicting situations with them in the future: Keep quiet, don't argue, and go ahead to do what I was resolved to do. My mum found this attribute of mine unsettling because no one could see it coming. I now know that this attribute of mine is called a passive-aggressive approach. A lot of my friends went with a risk-averse approach, choosing subjects that gave them a wide range of options for degree courses in university. However, I stuck with the exact subjects required to pursue a degree in engineering.

I let everyone know about my plans to study engineering in university. The adults around me thought I should take a less risky approach. They reasoned, why not go for a less demanding course, one with a lower cut-off mark so you would get admission into university on your first application? Some of them insinuated that engineering was a male-dominated field, and I would be competing against brilliant boys, making my chances of admission very slim. Overwhelmed by all this negative information, I changed my first and second choices on the application from engineering to any other degree courses I could find that had the same subject requirements but required lower marks for admission.

The universe always has a way to watch out for you. I say this because when I was finally admitted to study industrial chemistry, I became restless. I was busy telling friends how I still wanted to study engineering. I was among the top ten students on the admission list, and I would have easily been admitted to study engineering.

I recall this experience with mixed feelings because through this unfortunate situation, I learned a priceless life lesson that still guides me today: Do what you are convinced of and learn to shield off the noise. There is power in your instincts. You carry the dream and, hence, you have the power. Let no one take that from you. I go for goals that others find risky, unreasonable, or too high. They represent my convictions to hold and my dreams to protect.

Why Do You Want to Study Engineering?

While writing this book, I received a phone call from an old friend from my undergraduate years at the University of Nigeria, Nsukka. As we chatted, I recalled the wonderful memories I had of studying in school.

During my first year at the university, I found out that I could change departments, and so I could still reach my engineering dream. It was common practice to meet with the head of the desired department to indicate your interest. I showed up frequently to meet with Dr. Osuagwu, an older lecturer who was quite approachable. He always asked me, "Why do you want to change to engineering?" My answers ranged from wanting to change the world to wanting to build robots. At that time, I couldn't understand his need to ask me the same question time and time again. He liked to sneak the question in after pleasantries. I wondered if I was giving him the wrong answers. Did I not sound convincing enough?

Months down the line, I decided to cut my losses and just continue with industrial chemistry. Maybe the naysayers were right; I needed to be pragmatic. While waiting in Dr. Osuagwu's office, I had watched distinguished engineering professors and other highly accomplished dignitaries file in and out. How was I expected to compete with them—me, a young, fragile-looking teenager, dressed like a nerd but with fire in her eyes?

Roughly six weeks before exams, I was walking past the engineering department when Dr. Osuagwu stopped me. He was disappointed that he had not seen his "good friend" for weeks. He led me into his office and asked about my disappearance. I reeled out various excuses. He then brought out a course outline for engineering and handed it to me. "Your name has been on the board for weeks. You are now in second-year engineering," he informed me. I was perplexed and grateful. My mind wandered off while he explained what I needed to do. All I remembered were his last words, "You need to give me a first class" (in other words, get the highest honours degree).

I was amused. Was he joking, or did he really believe I could do it? Well, that was the beginning of one of the most amazing mentoring experiences I have had. Whenever I stopped by his office with my friend Esther, Dr. Osuagwu would remind us that we owed him a first-class honours degree. I later came to see this as a sign of his confidence and belief in my abilities. I felt that he saw the real me.

Dr. Osuagwu remains one of the people I am most grateful to, for his role during that phase in my journey.

> That incident taught me to always seek to understand "my why." The German philosopher Friedrich Nietzsche once said, "He who has a why can endure any how." Why are you trying to achieve a particular goal or dream? If you can fully understand this, your self-awareness empowers you to be focused and convinced about it. When you discover your why, it evolves to an understanding of who you really are. You can fully embrace the person you discover, or you can choose to more fully develop this person, if you believe the why is rooted in shallow, vain, or skewed desires. The main anchor here is that the power to change lies within you. A clear sense of purpose enables you to focus your efforts on what matters most, compelling you to take risks and push forward regardless of odds and obstacles, according to Margie Warrell (a columnist for *Forbes* and a media commentator).

Another important life lesson that I learned concerns the need to protect your dreams. The older people around me had reasons why they thought my goal was audacious, difficult, or wrong for my gender. There will always be people who do not buy into your dream, but your ability to fight for your dream is the key you need. The journey toward your dream will be filled with hurdles and naysayers. Challenges are part of the process. The outcome of navigating this process will include the building of your character. Your ability to push through builds resilience.

Dr. Osuagwu was a progressive lecturer during a time when lecturing was mainly about passing out information to students. He wanted his students involved and in the driver's seat of the learning experience. He wanted us to convert information into knowledge. He appointed students to research particular topics and then present their findings in the next class before he began lectures. I was always eager to be called upon, and I earnestly looked forward to giving the presentations that formed part of his class. He also invited graduates of the department to share their experiences in the workforce, and they offered insights about requirements for working in the industry.

I find that things that seemed rather unimportant in those days are now my strongest skills—communication, public speaking, teaching, storytelling, and the courage to be visible.

Getting a Foot in the Door

After graduating from university, I spent more than three months walking around Lagos looking for a job. Three months sounds like a short time now, but the anxiety and fear that drove me made it seem like forever. Every morning, I asked for transport fare from my dad, who was not working and still struggling to feed the family. The guilt and shame would kill me. I had been told, "Get a degree, and you will get a job." What they did not tell me was that jobs were not just waiting for you.

Living in an environment in which most people did not have a chance to get an education left me with few mentors or role models. Hope became a priceless asset because there was no one to show me the ropes. I leaned on a small group of people I had bonded with in "the jungle" who, like me, were seeking a way out of poverty via education. We shared similar desires for reassurance and direction. We were dreamers, encouraging each other and holding ourselves accountable.

I noticed that the biggest hurdles to cross in my job-hunting campaign were the security guards and gatemen at the establishments to which I wanted access. They quickly turned you back if you had no clue who you wanted to meet in the company. After a couple of failed attempts, I put together my go-to list of titles. I asked for the human resource manager, operations manager, or administration officer. In some cases, I got a "yes," and in other cases, I was shown the door out. But I kept at it. One time, I almost fainted at the bus stop due to what I now know was a heat stroke. I didn't want to give up. I was so scared. I felt my entire family was banking on me.

My friend Tina told me about a firm that was one of the best engineering companies in terms of its experience in the field and its pay for employees. I visited that office so many times that the receptionist eventually caved in. One day, she looked at me and said, "Today you will go home, but when you come back on Monday, just walk straight to me and ask for Mr. Lanre Kolade. I will let him know he has a guest waiting. Let him know you need a job, that you were referred to him, and make sure not to quote me."

I ran with the script and showed up on Monday, wearing my best suit and a lapel pin of the Institute of Electrical and Electronic Engineers (IEEE). It was my visual selling point for my competence. I spent a great deal of time trying to convince Lanre about my skills and competence, and he kept questioning me about who directed me to him. I kept evading the question, while pressing on about my abilities to deliver. He eventually told me to go upstairs for a quick chat with HR, and that started my interview process as an intern with Spar Aerospace.

Lanre was both driven and supportive. He gave me my first proper job as an engineer. These days when I meet him at industry meetings, I go all out to share my appreciation for him because he had faith in one determined girl who cold-called him. As my way of promoting this type of kindness, I am always eager to help others who approach me in a similar manner.

It is interesting to note that a few weeks before I was hired by Spar Aerospace, I had considered taking a job as a security guard. After weeks of searching for a job with no luck, one of my uncles offered to assist me with an opening for a security guard position. I was at such a low point that I actually considered taking it up. I had become acquaintances with a few of the guards at the establishments I visited during by job hunting, and I guess I thought it didn't seem like such a bad job. I don't recall what exactly happened with that possibility, but I assume it was overtaken by events, and I did not make it to the security guard recruitment exercise.

You might be wondering why a graduate of an engineering program would sell herself short. That is one of the biggest challenges of the slum—the development of low self-esteem or a lack of belief in your capabilities or in the system in general. When people in your extended circle are cooks, janitors, nannies, security guards, and so on—when people around you are just working hard to exist and make it to the next day—the desire to get more from life is inconsequential. As an ambitious individual wanting to change your situation, you tend to be a lonely dreamer, seeking what has eluded many. But I definitely do not belittle people who do the jobs I mentioned; neither do I look down on them. I understand that some people are employed in such jobs because the system gave them no chance. Perhaps no one believed in them enough or gave them access to push for their dreams.

Lanky is Leaving

As I write this, Lanky Bright (let's call him that), a tall, slim, and pleasant teenager I met at my workplace, is leaving for university. I have mixed emotions about this. I will miss his smiling face and polite manners as he cleans my office. He is one youth I have taken a particular interest in. But there are others. There have also been Esther, Abraham, Emeka, Chidinma, and Jide, to name a few. Our interactions have resulted in mentorship, and, in some cases, sponsoring them to school or assisting them in getting a job.

Most of these young people were initially surprised, uncomfortable, or suspicious about my interest in them and their ambitions. At first, Lanky rejected advice from me, insisting that he was okay with his salary. But he eventually admitted that he had greater ambitions. My exchanges with these individuals typically start with me seeing them reading a book (I am drawn to books). Then I start a conversation about the book, their interests, and their goals. I can be very intrusive when I choose to be, and my husband can attest to this. Most of these youth are office cleaners or security guards in our offices. Any one of them could have been Jane twenty years ago.

I have made a pact with myself to always try to give people a chance or a boost, especially when they are determined to break out of the poverty cycle through hard work and education. Alone, I cannot change the world. But I am willing to positively influence my immediate environment one person at a time. I see my career as an escalator journey. The height I have achieved so far gives me a platform to meet amazing talents, as well as an opportunity to give back as much as I can.

CHAPTER 4

The Corporate Escalator

In 2009, I was passed over for a certain promotion twice. What confused me more than that was the fact that the candidates chosen for the promotion were colleagues whom I felt were far less qualified than me. The role was in sales. I knew the customers, I had built the relationships, and I was closing the deals. Strangely enough, I had helped train some of the candidates who were now being promoted above me. After much reflection, I decided to confront my boss. I wanted to know what skill sets he was looking for to fill the next role, how I measured up, and what areas he thought I should work on. I even recommended a quarterly review feedback meeting with him. It was in one of those feedback sessions that he told me, as I walked out of his office, "Jane, your career is in your hands." I looked back, bemused. How dare he say that? If I had the power, I should have been promoted by now!

Your Career is in Your Hands

There will always be bias in corporate organisations. What is important is your response to these types of situations. What do you do?

After many meetings and a couple of failed attempts to send me to other departments, my boss could see I was restless. I was not giving up on my goal of being promoted to the next open management position. He arranged for me to meet the vice president of human resources during her next visit to Nigeria. I thought, finally someone is listening. Maybe she will help sort things out for me.

The HR VP was an American lady in her fifties who had run her own human resources consultancy practice before returning to the corporate world. She was feisty, blunt, and forward. I loved that—a woman with guts. I walked into her office respectfully and introduced myself. We spoke casually about my career journey so far, including the positions I had had in the past.

> "Jane, I can see that for several years these promotions have all been lateral moves. You have had no upward movement," she told me.
>
> I was happy to hear that. At least here was someone who understood me. My career journey had been stagnating, and no one was addressing it.
>
> She went on, "For the next role you desire and going forward in your career movement upward, it will be ninety-percent network and one-percent talent."

Now she really had my attention. I wanted to hear more. Maybe she held the answers. I leaned in as I sat across from her.

"Each time you walk in a room desiring these management positions, the fact that you are female, black, and married with kids is working against you."

That hit me hard. I couldn't fully understand what she was saying. What did all that have to do with my desire for a management role in a telecommunication company?

At the end of our meeting, I went home and ruminated over her statements. I wrote them in a journal. I discussed them with my close friends and my husband. I was trying to dissect what she had said, and I struggled with the reality of what she meant. Was she saying that because I was female, black, and married with kids, my career was over? Did she mean I did not have the right profile to grow in the organisation? Could it be that the company had turned a blind eye to managing bias in the organisation and ensuring that decision-makers promote staff based on the right attributes rather than their own prejudices?

I finally decided that if the company was unwilling to promote me because of the unconscious bias that exists in our male-dominated field and industry, I would heed my boss's advice and take my career in my own hands. I resigned. And I took a job with a direct competitor. That was how, in 2010, I left a company where I had worked for almost eight years. It was a bittersweet experience, and my first realization that there would always be bias in my field. Decision-makers are human beings with baggage and biases, and in a company where this is left unchecked, a negative environment for diversity in management will be created.

> Some people will think you are too young, too old, or have the wrong gender for a role. When we allow social stereotypes about gender, race, sexual orientation, age, or other personal characteristics to influence decisions subconsciously, it is called unconscious bias. Such bias typically forms outside our awareness, and it involves attributing particular qualities to members of certain social groups. Most people are, in one way or another, influenced by the implicit biases that are shrouded in our environment, culture, and religious beliefs.

Christine Jolls and Cass R. Sunstein, in their analysis of the Implicit Association Test (IAT), state that implicit bias is largely automatic. They mean that the characteristic in question (skin color, age, or sexual orientation) operates so quickly, as seen in the relevant tests, that people have no time to deliberate. It is for this reason that people are often surprised to find that they show the implicit bias.

In my case, the selection process was left to the subjective decision of the line manager in charge. His implicit bias led him to assume that because I was a black female who was married with kids, it might be difficult for me to manage a multinational team, meet the travel requirements of the job, and put in the effort and commitment that the job required.

One way in which companies can avoid this pitfall is to clearly articulate the requirements for a role and demand that line managers adhere to those requirements when evaluating candidates. During a training session on unconscious biases that Google's Director of People Analytics, Dr. Brian Welle, gave to a group of company founders, he indicated that his company's use of specific criteria and standardized questions prevents managers from making biased hiring decisions. "The lesson," he said, "is that it's important to articulate the exact things Google is looking for in every position it fills."

Speak Up, Ask, and Ask Again

I have learned that you mostly get what you ask for in life, so you must also apply this lesson to your career. Only in very few cases are you simply handed promotions and responsibilities. My personal experience is that you need to be ready to ask for what you want. There are no guarantees you will receive it immediately, but at least you have sent the message to your employers or management staff that you have a desire to grow, and seek more responsibility.

So, as I mentioned, I left a company because I felt I was being passed over for promotions. Well, this same company came calling for me two years after I left. Following nine months of "courtship" and negotiations, I returned on my own terms. My new boss was Turkish, young, smart, and very ambitious. He believed I was key to helping him close a major deal. I made it clear to him that I would take on the new role for one year, and I needed to be promoted or leave the unit after that. I was in control. I set the terms, and boy, did I stick to them!

One year later, after closing the deal as agreed, I learned that my boss was being promoted to work in another country. During a follow-up meeting about my career ambitions, I reminded him of my conditions for taking the role and returning to the Organisation. I had met all his requirements for the promotion, but he had not yet kept his side of the agreement. Surprisingly after our chat, the promotion came faster than I'd expected. I was promoted to a new management position and sent to Ghana. That is the power of asking and being in control of your career.

> I have discovered that most of the attitudes we are taught as females are contrary to what is expected in the workplace. We are groomed to be fine ladies, waiting for a guy to ask us out or request our hand in marriage. To a large extent, being forward is not seen as an acceptable feminine virtue. But in the workplace, you are expected to speak up, ask for what you want, and be clear about your expectations of others. And you have to do this in a field that is male-dominated and in a culture that promotes masculine attributes.

Having that chat with my new boss was very uncomfortable for me. I sat across the table from him, reminding him of my ambitions and goals and reiterating my achievements. I did not want to seem desperate. I had hoped he would acknowledge my work on his own, rather than requiring me to remind him of my achievements. Unfortunately, that is not how the game is played in the workplace.

I am now discovering the importance of teaching our kids and empowering them with the right skills to navigate the world and future corporate Organisations. For my daughters, I need to get across the idea that some of the female stereotypes propagated by society are outdated and unproductive.

There are No Enemies, Only Divergent Interests

The boss who passed me up for promotion twice, prompting me to leave the company, became one of my greatest sponsors after I returned. In fact, he was instrumental in arranging for me to go to Ghana for the management job.

When I first returned to the company, I attended a strategy session in South Africa, where he and I ended up sitting at the same table during the evening session. During one of the informal chat sessions, he asked how I was faring. He wanted to know how I saw the Organisation now, after having worked for the competition. I initially gave some standard responses, but I then brought his attention to the fact that the Organisation was making it difficult to promote women. We had very few women in line management positions (typically the first rung on the management ladder). Capable women were assumed to have put their careers on hold after they married and started having children. They were not being given additional responsibility or offered line management positions. Many of these women were leaving the Organisation. When I mentioned these points to him, I did not intend for them to be anything more than frank remarks.

Later that night, he approached me to let me know that there was a line management role available in another country. He thought I would be a good fit. He shared details about the head of the unit and insisted that I have a chat with him to sell my skills and experience before I left the strategy session. During the session, he insisted that I sit at the front of the table. Normally, I sat at the back. Overall, he behaved in a manner that conflicted with my negative perceptions of him.

He didn't stop there. He gave me details about management deliberations and pointed out the members of the executive team who were unsure of my abilities. Most of the executive management staff did not know me personally. He encouraged me to prepare to pitch to them and recommended the best time to do so. It seemed like a campaign to sell Jane to the management team.

This is where most women struggle and why we need sponsors. Sponsors help you advance in your career, but many female employees find it difficult to develop sponsor relationships. A sponsor is someone with power who is senior to you, knows your work, and takes active steps to help you advance. That individual might introduce you to influential connections, highlight your work to senior leaders, or recommend you for jobs and promotions.

Employees with sponsors are 1.4 times more likely to say they've had a meaningful interaction with a senior leader and 1.5 times more likely to aspire to be a top executive themselves[8]—and this is especially true for women. Yet, fewer than one in four employees has a sponsor.[9] Hence, they do not have anyone talking them up to senior management and putting personal capital behind them.

I worried about my former boss's sudden interest in me getting a promotion. Why the attention and support? Why now? I finally discovered that he had been made the head of the diversity and inclusion board of the Organisation, and it was his goal to seek out top performers for management roles among underrepresented groups. The company was seeking to have 33-percent female representation at the management level within five years, but it was currently barely at 5 percent.

I do not subscribe entirely to the quota system because I believe that women should be given responsibilities based on their merit. The quota system might not be sustainable, and it can sometimes result in tokenism and moral licensing. Moral licensing creates a ripple effect when Organisations believe that, having met a certain female quota, they do not need to do more. As Malcolm Gladwell, the Canadian journalist and author puts it, "You open the door to one outsider now and this gives you permission to close the door to others."[10] However, I do recognize that a quota system might be required in some situations to give women their first chance at a seat at a particular table. It can break open the door, allowing women access to roles traditionally dominated by men, and force firms to be aware of addressing the gaps.

A big lesson I took away from this experience is that there are no enemies; there are only people with different interests. When we have shared interests and agendas, things work well for the parties involved. This complex situation should not be the ideal, especially

---

[8] (krivkovich *et al.*, 2018).

[9] (krivkovich *et al.*, 2018).

[10] (Gladwell, 2016).

in the corporate world. However, Organisations are not ideal, and human beings will always possess goals tainted by their own agendas. As you walk along your career journey, learn to have no strings attached, and understand that quick wins come more easily when we look for areas with shared interests.

Take Risks

I agree with Helen Keller that life is either a daring adventure or nothing at all.[11] The truth is that your career journey will sometimes demand that you take risks or attempt things that scare you or make you uncomfortable. Your ability to take on the challenge and dare to follow the adventure can sometimes have immense rewards. If you are prepared and seize the opportunities, you make it to the other side with great success. That's assuming you have defined what success means to you.

Taking risks is no easy feat. On this particular occasion, it gave me fulfillment, and the process took me to a new level regarding how I saw my career. The experience fed a part of me that desired meaningful work, work that influenced others, and work that reached out for a greater good. I took pride in what my Organisation stood for, and I desired to develop my career in that particular company.

In the words of Jeffrey A. Sonnenfeld and Andrew J. Ward, the authors of *Firing Back: How Great Leaders Rebound After Career Disasters*, "No one can truly define success and failure for us—only we can define that for ourselves. No one can take away our dignity unless we surrender it. No one can take away our hope and pride unless we relinquish them. No one can steal our creativity, imagination, and skills unless we stop thinking. No one can stop us from rebounding unless we give up."[12]

---

[11] (Keller, 1957)

[12] (Sonnenfeld et al., 2007)

CHAPTER 5

EGERTON AND I

I sat on the edge of the bed as he stood across the room staring at me. Waiting. He wanted answers to his questions, and he was not letting go. A million thoughts ran through my mind. I quickly analyzed my options on how best to respond: tell the truth or deflect the issue. Surprising myself, I burst out crying. He let me cry; he was patient.

I blurted out, "You know that job I always wanted, the one I interviewed for? Well, now they are saying if I am to get it, I will have to do it in Ghana." I sat there vulnerable, voicing my fears and concerns. I laid it all out there for him. Acknowledging his recent promotion, I said, "You have just gotten promoted to a very senior role in one of the biggest multinationals in Nigeria, and I know what it took you to get that role, Egerton. Our son is finally in the school we always wanted after being on a two-year waiting list. Despite my many travels, this country is one I have never been to, and I don't think I know anyone who lives there."

I told Egerton I suspected that I might have been set up—that the company was looking for ways to get me to reject the position. Why recommend me for a role in a country I had not applied for? When I brought this concern to the attention of the recruiters, I was told that the role I had applied for was in a larger market—that is, a larger country—but they wanted me to apply for the same role in a smaller market. The job offer came after the company had claimed for weeks that it did not even receive my application for the position. I was called for a meeting about the position only after forwarding the automatic response generated by the system, sending several emails inquiring about the position, and resending my CV. I believed that the company knew it would be tougher for me to relocate, and I was likely to reject the proposed position in Ghana. How was I going to move with my kids and husband to another country if I got the job? In most situations within my patriarchal Nigerian environment and the male-dominated telecommunication industry, the man takes the expatriate role, not the woman.

I felt better after sharing all these concerns with Egerton. I had bottled it all up for too long. The simple question Egerton had asked me that day, prompting my emotional outburst, was, "Baby, what's the matter? Something is clearly bothering you. You have been snapping at everyone for weeks, and we are all walking on eggshells around you."

I have never forgotten Egerton's words after I poured my heart out to him. I was pleasantly surprised. I never thought it would play out that way, not even in my wildest dreams. Egerton told me that he wanted a happy marriage, and he knew that to achieve this, his wife needed to be happy. He said that he understood my career was important to me and that achieving this milestone would mean a lot for me. So he was going to support me. He encouraged me to go ahead and apply for the position in Ghana.

"If you get the role, we can work out the details on how to make it work with time," he reassured me.

Partnership

In June 2016, while I was working and living with my kids in Ghana, my husband took unpaid study leave for a year. It happened like this. Egerton had taken some days off work to spend an extended weekend with the family in Ghana. One morning, as I was dashing off to work, he said, "Baby, I need us to talk about this master's stuff, the one I sent you the flier about. We need to make a decision." I thought it was going to be a quick discussion. I was not actually listening as I sat next to him at the dining table fumbling with my phone.

"Jane, I need you to listen."

I put away my phone and started querying him about his interest in doing the master's programme in faraway Asia, expressing my reservations about the school because of the cost of the programme. That led to both of us agreeing that we needed to do some research about the programme. I took my just-do-it approach and suggested that we email the school immediately to ask the questions we had, and that he call a colleague who had completed the programme to discuss its value. Then I headed off to work.

By the end of that day, based on all the responses we had received, the tables switched. I was the one trying to convince Egerton that our family could handle the financial strain that came with such a commitment.

So he went to Singapore to undertake the master's programme. The total cost of the programme was similar to costs at Ivy League schools in the United States, and there were also extra travel costs. After we gathered our savings to pay the fees, our family would have to survive on my paycheck alone for the entire year that Egerton was studying for his master's degree. This meant keeping a tight leash on our expenses, cutting out luxuries (like summer vacation and other family trips), and putting a hold on all our investments.

The time zone difference meant I had to stay up late on most nights after a hard day's work to talk with him. Video chats were our standard form of communication, and on most mornings, the kids joined in to chat with their dad on their way to school. Because Egerton no longer made weekend trips to Ghana, I was their only parent at home physically. I missed the support he had given during those times, and during the times when he stayed with our kids while I went on long business trips. I missed his emotional support. Egerton had been a line manager long before I was, and he had managed far larger teams than I had. I found his perspective priceless when it came to people management. The time difference meant we had to be patient with one another, and the short time slot we had to talk meant that we prioritized what we discussed.

Egerton's programme ended in mid-2017. It proved to be very beneficial to my husband's career as well as to his personal development. He was grateful and proud of my support during that phase of our lives.

> Being supportive, communicative, and vulnerable with each other makes our partnership work. Our society encourages women to sacrifice all for their marriage and family even if it means giving up their voice, dreams, and entire purpose. I believe that marriage is a partnership. When it comes to sacrifice and compromise, each partner needs to chip in. Resentment and burnout builds if one partner is always on the giving end and not receiving support in the things that matter most to him or her. I am so grateful to be in a marriage where my partner is willing to sacrifice and support my dreams, and I seek to do the same for him. This for me is invaluable.

Egerton and I have both taken turns to manage the home front when one of us needed to travel alone for business or pleasure. We take turns to not only manage the home front, but also to offer emotional support to each other. I recall one trip in which I was away from home for three weeks—one week at my London head office for meetings, the next week in the U.S. for leadership training at the Yale School of Management, and the last week in South Africa for customer meetings. Egerton took our daughter for every ballet class on the weekends, oversaw the kids' homework, and ensured he was physically present for them. In between my trips, I had a free weekend and decided to check out a museum in Boston on my own.

We love to visit museums as a family. So my husband and I arranged a virtual tour of the museum for the kids via a video call. I showed them the Nigerian artifacts in the museum while he explained the history and importance of Nigerian culture to them. It was a bonding experience for us, though I was miles away. Sharing and connecting with my family despite the distance between us made me feel so loved.

I believe that once each partner is willing to sacrifice for the other, then the receiving partner is in a safer place to do likewise in the future. This is somewhat like the "emotional bank account" discussed in Stephen R. Covey's book, *The 7 Habits of Highly Effective People.* Each partner has an emotional bank account for the other. The more we give and support our partner, the more we make deposits in our account with him or her. This assumes that the partner is aware of our deposits and acknowledges them. Once we make these deposits, it should be easier to make withdrawals in the future. My point is not that we keep scores and check who is making deposits, but we need to understand that in a partnership everyone brings something to the table. It takes both partners giving, to make it work.

In Bed with the Customer

While I was a sales manager at a multinational telecom, my company needed to resolve some issues with a customer, and the key contact person in the customer's Organisation called for a meeting. All the main stakeholders in the Organisation were invited. I sat in a boardroom with several very disappointed and dissatisfied customers. We had sold them a crucial product that was not delivering any of the functions we promised, and they were finding it difficult to monetize the product.

All of us in the room had different agendas for the day. My team and I were there to listen to their complaints and hopefully seek ways to redress this disaster. The customers were there to voice their concerns, listing their problems and expecting us to share solutions in the meeting. We reaffirmed that we would take their concerns back to our office and deliberate on solutions internally. We would then share the next steps for addressing the issue.

I noticed that one particular customer in the meeting was resistant to our efforts to assuage their concerns. As is usual in such contentious meetings, I had introduced myself to members of the customer's Organisation whom I was meeting for the first time, and I gave them my business card. That was how I met Egerton. He was the difficult customer that kept pushing for answers.

I oversaw the process of rebuilding the customers' confidence in that product. I flew in a couple of specialists from our global team to Lagos to run workshops for stakeholders within their Organisation. At the workshops, we addressed all issues regarding the use of the product, its features, and monetization. During the break times, we all stepped out of the boardroom for fresh air.

One such time, I noticed a group of stakeholders standing together while some smoked in their midst, but Egerton stood alone, away from the group. I walked up to him, enquiring why he did not join the others. He said that he did not smoke and second-hand smoke affected him. I knew that most of the guys at the workshop chose to join the group because their bosses were part of it. So I thought, this guy has a mind of his own; he chose to stand apart. That was when I really noticed him, and we chatted for a bit.

Weeks later, I walked into my office on a Friday morning, wondering what I was going to do that day because I had already achieved my main goals for the week. I said a quick prayer, "God, guide me to achieve something today."

Then it suddenly occurred to me that I had promised to share more product materials with Egerton, and some of them needed to be installed with special software. His office was in Apapa, on Lagos

Mainland. I usually tried to avoid that part of town during working hours because of the immense traffic. A round trip required over three hours. However, I rationalized that I had nothing to lose on that day because I had nothing else to do. I got an official car and driver and headed to his office.

After submitting the materials, I bantered with him a bit, so I could get to know him better. I usually did this with customers. I asked him what he did on weekends. He brought out a duffel bag from under his table and started to unload the books from within. The first book that fell out was a worn, brown, leather Bible, followed by several management books.

"This is what I do. I read," he said.

I was amused and curious. What a focused individual. The more we chatted, the more I was attracted to him. I love intellectually minded people. I asked him questions about his work and social life. When he did not fully understand my question or viewpoint, he asked for clarity. He seemed to genuinely want to understand and engage in the discussion with me. His thoughtful responses seemed as though they came from a place of self-awareness and sincereness.

"Would you like to go dancing with me sometime?" I asked.

He looked surprised, and then mumbled some excuse about not being a good dancer. I explained that it was a ballroom dance class. No matter your level, you could learn to dance. Moreover, after classes, participants danced for a couple of hours before the sessions ended. It was so much fun and kept me busy on weekends. He didn't give me a firm yes, but as he walked me to my car, he promised to call me sometime.

Halfway to my office, I called him. "I just wanted to update you. I'm halfway to my office."

I am smiling as I write this. I mean, who does that? The next call from him started the road to a six-month courtship that resulted in us getting married about a year later.

I Have My Voice

Elaine Rose enumerates some truths in her article, "Does Education Really Disadvantage Women in the Marriage Market?" She writes that the last several decades have seen profound changes in the roles of women in the labour market and the family. Both media reports and academic research tend to emphasize the conflict that women face between their roles in these two spheres. One recurring theme is the "success penalty," referring to the disadvantage that career success poses to women in the marriage market. Career women are seen as less submissive by potential husbands and lacking the ability to be nurturing of others. They are further viewed as lacking the ability to have it all—career, marriage, and family.

I believe our discussions should move beyond the ideas of a woman needing financial aid or holding a job solely for financial objectives. We need to progress to the point where a woman's partner understands that she has desires to explore the world and prove herself. Women in relationships are not commodities with expected duties and responsibilities. In patriarchal societies like mine, husbands, in-laws, parents, relatives, and friends set those expectations. It is important that early in the relationship, both parties respect the fact that each individual has his or her desires, ambitions, and expectations. It is also important to communicate these early on and be open to support each other.

You might ask, how does a young woman develop the courage to be this way in a society that doesn't encourage her? I would say a great sign is the fact that you are able to discuss this freely with whomever you are dating. You need to have an open conversation about this, no matter how difficult it may be. Although not foolproof, the ability to have such a conversation could give an early indication of how aligned both parties are. It may also open up a deeper discussion about the willingness to support each other's journey.

Early in our relationship, one thing that stood out was the respect that Egerton accorded me. He wanted to know my thoughts on key issues, and he wanted key decisions to be made jointly by both of us. We planned together and were equal participants in creating our future. He would not impose his opinion, and he accepted the superior argument, even if it came from me. I had a voice that mattered as much as my partner's voice.

When my friend Lynda called me into her office and asked me why I liked Egerton, my exact words were, "He treats me like a queen."

My Career, My Marriage

My career is important to me because it is a platform I use to express my desire to live to my full potential. I try to use this platform to inspire and influence my community positively. It is more than a job to me. I am not driven by the material benefits that come with developing my career, but by the satisfaction that comes from breaking doors and pushing boundaries. I have decided that these two important things in my life—my career and my family—will receive my full attention and commitment. They nurture and push me to enjoy my journey on Earth.

> The question for society is, why are women asked to make a binary choice when we consider marriage and career? This question arises when social barriers, like the "glass ceiling," are used to describe women's career challenges. The binary choice is insinuated by the lack of public policies to support women during maternity, as well as by social conditioning that ascribes certain careers as preferred choices for women. But shouldn't careers be matters of prioritization? Once the priorities and the perspective are clear, then the choice of where a woman directs her attention at any particular second is left to her to consider and act on.

My thoughts on this issue are perfectly captured by Daenerys in the *Game of Thrones* series: "I'm not going to stop the wheel; I'm going to break the wheel." Daenerys decided that her purpose was to stop the way the vulnerable were being taken advantage of by powerful families.[13] We need to break the wheel of thought suggesting that women need to choose between being a mother/housewife and having a career.

[13] (Craven, 2019).

CHAPTER 6

Motherhood and Birth Stories

I wanted to have all my babies within two years of each other and then settle back into my career. However, three years after my first son, Asher, was born, becoming pregnant again seemed difficult. My gynaecologist waved off my persistent requests for assisted fertility options. He suggested that maybe my lifestyle was making pregnancy difficult because my job involved frequent travel. I was tired of stalling my career, avoiding new challenges, and waiting to have babies through a process that I seemingly had little control over. But women who want children while developing their careers face these challenges. The impact of the decision on when to have kids for working families is much less intrusive on the careers of men.

I decided to take the plunge. Why stall when I could further develop my career? I started seeking job opportunities outside my company. At the same time, my doctor finally agreed to commence some light hormonal fertility treatment with me. A couple of months after stopping my fertility treatments, I took on bigger responsibilities in a new Organisation—and then I found out I was pregnant. How was I supposed to explain this to my new boss? The anxiety created by my situation almost destroyed the joy of knowing I carried new life within me.

Having children affects your career as a woman. Motherhood can bring fulfilment, and it can teach and inspire us. On the flip side, combining this role with a career can be daunting and demanding.

In one phase of my career, I served on the diversity and inclusion board of my employer, Ericsson, a Fortune-500 company in the telecommunication industry. This was a nonprofit board set up to help create an environment in which diversity thrives. During the board meetings, we quickly realized that one of our main challenges was not a pipeline problem (lack of women starting careers in science, engineering, technology, or mathematics), but a leakage problem. We were losing women as their careers advanced. Most women left the Organisation, and some changed careers, after they married and started raising families.

> Why were these women abandoning their careers? How could organisations (including private companies, public-sector institutions, and non-profits and policy makers) better support women during this phase of their lives? Addressing the leakage problem could help Organisations retain some of their best talents, boosting productivity in the workplace. It is my hope that we can advance the discussion about this matter in these pages.

The Motherhood Penalty

The term "motherhood penalty" refers to the decline in women's career growth or the increase in the wage gap between men and women, both of which occur during the motherhood phase. Desi Lydic, in her Comedy Central show, *Womansplains*, notes that in the United States, certain lifestyle choices, like motherhood, create a wage gap between men and women. These women earn about 39 percent less than men. The wage gap is higher for women who have kids and lower for women who never have kids. She further explains that the motherhood penalty is a long-term financial hit that women have to deal with after taking time off, leaving a job, or working part-time in order to raise their kids.

I felt the impact of the motherhood penalty when I returned from my maternity leave after having my daughter, Sarah. I realized that the promotion I was in line for—and even positioned for by my immediate boss—had been given to someone else. This most likely happened because of my absence during the strategic time of the company's restructuring and reorganisation.

My pregnancy was an interesting journey for me. One particular experience during the early days remains etched in my memory. I was sitting in the consultation room across the table from my gynaecologist, Dr. Bero. He said, "Jane, you will need to slow down. I don't want you to lose this baby. Can you slow down on the foreign trips and rest more?" I smiled as he repeated the last sentence for emphasis. It was not a smile of acceptance; it was a closed-lip smile. It was my way of telling him that he did not get it.

A couple of days earlier, I had woken up abruptly at about 4 a.m. It was dark because we had no electrical power. (Nigeria is known for its electrical power problems.) Egerton was not in the bedroom. We had had one of those quarrels that sends one partner to the guest room. I slowly walked across to the guest room and knocked on the door, not sure what was going on with my body. I asked Egerton to kindly switch on the power generator, so we could turn the lights on. I was wet, and I didn't know why. Trepidation and tension filled the air as Egerton quickly switched on the generator. Only then did we realize my nightgown was soaked with my blood. I was a couple of weeks pregnant with my daughter.

Egerton called our family doctor, Dr. Akere, explaining the situation. Dr. Akere recommended that I lie down and then come to the hospital at the break of dawn. Egerton and I had one of the longest waits of our lives. He cleaned the blood spots on the floor and tucked me into bed when I began to shiver. In the morning, all we wanted was reassurance that our baby was okay. Dr. Akere showed us an ultrasound scan of the baby swimming in her amniotic fluid, oblivious to the panic that Egerton and I had gone through early that morning.

Looking at Dr. Bero as he reiterated the need for me to slow down, I almost screamed, "Tell me how to do that!" I was four months into a new job when I found out I was pregnant. Like most management roles in a new Organisation, my first hundred days were crucial. I worked hard to prove myself, and I tried to hide the fact that I was pregnant. The day before the bleeding incident, my boss had visited from Dubai. After more than four back-to-back meetings with clients all over the city, which involved climbing stairs, I started to feel sharp pains in my abdomen. I ignored them, hoping that with some rest I would get better in the morning. But it was not to be.

A month after this bleeding incident, I sought advice from the head of human resources. She informed me that I was eligible for maternity leave because I would have spent a year with the company by the time I would need the leave. I also had to inform my boss, who thankfully accepted the situation. The experience was, nevertheless, very traumatic for my family.

I had pushed myself hard during that pregnancy because my boss let me know that there were plans to move me to a higher role if I continued at that pace. I was to assume the new role once I returned from maternity leave. According to Nigerian labour law, official maternity leave is three months. I returned from my leave to an entirely different company structure and, because I was not there during the restructuring, I was barely clinging to my old job. I lost the promotion to a new colleague who had joined the Organisation as part of the acquisition. There were strong indications that if I was around during the restructuring, the situation might have been different. Out of sight can be out of mind for some Organisations.

The cost to women who decide to have children and remain in the workforce is real, and it is substantial. The danger of losing your baby in some cases, or of losing career opportunities or being sidelined are constant dilemmas that women have to face at this stage of their lives. Some motherhood penalties are exacerbated by the ways in which Organisations are run or by inadequate policies to support women during the childbearing phase. Making Organisations hospitable to women who have children is paramount to enable these employees to stay and grow in their careers. In some countries, including the United States, women are still clamouring for guaranteed paid maternity leave. We need to ensure that women on maternity leave are not written off from management roles during their leaves.

Loving Sarah

They say to be careful what you wish for because you might just get it. I have worked hard to develop my career but never realized that simple things can become an overwhelming challenge along the way. While some of the roadblocks in the motherhood phase are external, women also face internal and personal barriers.

When my daughter was about three, I was on the road every two weeks over a three-month period. When I finally settled back to my normal routine at home, I noticed that she would leave her room and run down the hallway to sleep in our live-in nanny's room every night. My room was next to my daughter's room. Every night, I read her a bedtime story, prayed with her, and kissed her good night. However, whenever she woke up, I heard her tiny steps dashing to the nanny's room instead of to me. I tried talking with her about it, making a case for why she should head to mummy first. This method worked with my older son, but it didn't work with my three-year-old daughter.

I reached out to seek advice from women with similar experiences. I poured my heart out to a very senior executive who had pursued a similar career path but now had grown kids. Her advice was priceless, and it has never left me: "You need to treat her the way you treat the most important clients you have. Carve out time for her, quality time, and keep trying to win her over no matter how long it takes."

The moment my goal of winning Sarah back started to yield results was the first night she ran to my room when she had a nightmare. I smiled as tears welled up in my eyes. It was an indescribable feeling, better than closing a hundred-million-dollar deal. I kept saying to myself that night, "She chose me!" Yes!

Since that day, I have treated Sarah as my top client. No matter how tired I am, my nightly routine with her stands. I cancelled my cycling on Saturdays to take her to weekly ballet sessions. I now braid her hair to bond with her, though I am barely good at it. We also bond over her toys and dressing up. I seek ways to volunteer in her class. When we can, we catch a movie together, though at the last one, I was so tired that I slept during parts of it. This has been the biggest deal I have closed so far! I think it took me almost nine months to come to the point of sharing this story without guilt over the experience haunting me.

> This is not the kind of challenge that a government policy or an Organisation can directly resolve. It is one that mentoring and peer support can address, and I strongly recommend that women on similar journeys be aware of it. I see Organisations facilitating avenues for this support within their structures, by making available coaching resources and tools that can assist women.

I have learned to reprioritise my goals on my career journey, acknowledging that my path is different from that of my mother and other women in the past who sought a balanced life and were good at it all: marriage, family, and career. I have also learned from Frances Frei, a professor at Harvard Business School, that I should *dare to be bad.*

Frei talks about *uncommon service,* in which you dare to be bad at some things, so you can be great at other things. In other words, as a woman you can't be a perfect career woman, perfect mother, and perfect wife. Some things will slip, but you have to decide what things should be given the right attention and priority. You can't be good at everything, so have the courage to be bad at some things! I will be bad at domestic activities such as cooking and cleaning, so I can spend quality time with my family. There are seasons where I am bad at social engagements or hosting friends, so I can be present with my family on weekends. I found Frei's advice to be profound and liberating.

This can be a definition of success.

The Motherhood Bonus

The motherhood journey can be a very rewarding one. I am learning to embrace it, accepting this gift while creating harmony with my career. In doing so, I am inspired and motivated to be a better person. Motherhood gives me perspective and, in some cases, helps me to manage stress at work better.

At one point, I was going through a tough career transition, and after a couple of not-so-pleasant job interviews, I subconsciously gave up because of my negative experiences. I discarded one of my motivational phrases, which I use whenever I go for an interview, an exam, or some other assessment: "Own the room; don't let people project their insecurities or fears on you." An encounter with my daughter helped bring me back on course.

After one of my not-so-pleasant board interviews, I drove to her school to pick her up from her end-of-term party and take her to her violin practical exam. We arrived at the venue of the exam an hour before her allocated time. I let her catch a quick power nap, and then we dived into some revisions of her musical selections. We rosined her bow and tuned her violin. I even got her to play the scales and her selected pieces one more time. Then we headed to the exam building. As we climbed the stairs, I decided to give her a pep talk. My daughter was eight and new to the world of examinations because her school does not conduct exams for kids that age. Her only previous exam had taken place the year before—a music theory exam.

I reminded her, "Sarah, you know during this exam it will just be you playing for the examiner." She skipped up the stairs, smiling and looking happy as I continued. "You should not expect the examiner to like you, smile at you, or be happy with you. Please play your music pieces and answer the questions respectfully, this is serious!"

She danced on the landing and responded, "Mom, don't worry. I am going to play my pieces, and they will love it. The examiner will enjoy it and be happy."

I hurried after her as she took off. In the waiting room, I made one more attempt. I stooped down close to her seat, leaning into her. "Sarah, the examiner will be firm and keep a straight face."

She leaned toward me, and I could see the twinkle in her eyes as she asked, "Mom, will it be like the Mona Lisa face?"

"Yes, dear, it will be a poker face. The idea is not to give away the outcome of their assessment right away. Is that okay?"

Now she was swinging her feet, holding the sides of her seat as she said, "Mom, I told you they are going to love it when I play. They will be nice."

I caught a glimpse of the assistant coordinator smiling at us, and I felt others in the room staring and listening. I was not getting through to my daughter. She was all smiles and humming a song. I blamed it on sugar. She must have had too much sugary stuff at that party.

I had believed she needed a pep talk based on previous experience with my son, Asher. A year earlier, after he finished his music exam, he broke into tears when I asked him how it went. He had made a mistake while playing his piano pieces and had seen the examiner looking at him expressionlessly. He panicked and made more mistakes. Thank God he passed by a hair's breadth.

Reflecting on that day later, I realized that my anxiety over Sarah's exam could be attributed to the board interview I had that morning. When I was being interviewed for an executive position, I had struggled to decipher an interviewer's assessment of me. I suspected that he made comments to either unsettle me or indicate his bias. He started his questions by mentioning that he thought they already had a good candidate for the position. After that incident, I decided to prepare my daughter for a tough exam situation.

Sarah, however, was not having any of it. When she went in for the exam, I stood close to the door, trying to eavesdrop. I was so nervous that my heart skipped a bit when I thought she missed a note. I decided this was unhealthy and headed to the washroom. After what seemed like an eternity, my daughter emerged, smiling with a twinkle in her eyes and a rhythmic gait. I held her hands and bent over, asking how it went.

"Mom, it was excellent, the examiner loved it. I told you! I played my pieces, he asked me some questions, and even when he tried to make them tricky, I answered them. He nodded his head and said, 'good.' At the end, I told him he was nice, and he smiled, mommy."

I asked her to repeat what happened two more times as we walked back to the car. I tried to process what she told me. When we got inside the car I said, "Sarah, you are right. It is okay to smile and be happy and confident when you walk into an exam. You don't need to worry about how the examiner looks or feels. Maybe, in the end, you might infect him or her with your positive attitude. We must let Asher know this when we get home."

My daughter reminded me to maintain a positive attitude, especially in situations in which I am being assessed. I was learning from Sarah and, for me, this was a motherhood bonus. She brought my attention to the false assumptions we hold when we generalize our negative experiences and put a label on them, transferring them from one part of our lives to another. Sarah's outlook was the motivation and inspiration I needed to keep going at my interviews with a positive attitude.

> Children do not necessarily put their mothers at centre stage. Mothers do not always get validation or attention from their children. One way to deal with internally and externally exacerbated challenges during the motherhood phase is to get support from other women. Women also can become the problem solvers in their Organisations.

We shall explore the need to be the change we seek in subsequent chapters.

CHAPTER 7

It is Lonely at the Top

He filled the chair with no room to spare. Ben—let's call him that—was swinging slowly from side to side on one of those big executive chairs that spin. He tapped the table with his fingers quietly as he talked to me. He did not dress formally, as most of the other executives did, but preferred large-sized plaid shirts, which he did not bother tucking in, further exaggerating his build. Sitting across the table from him, I was leaning in, the very opposite in style. Always dressed in heels, I wore a plain-colored, slim-fitted dress. As my career grew I evolved from the tomboy look of my undergraduate days to a business formal dressing for work. I loved the clean and structured look. I tilted my head to the side, engrossed in the story he was telling me. Ben was an executive in my client's Organisation.

"When you get home today, Jane, I need you to fill a bucket to the brim with water. Once you have done so, dip your hand into the bucket of water and take it out. I need you to look into the bucket of water and see if taking your hand out creates a hole."

Initially I was bewildered. Later, I smiled to cover my amusement as I processed his riddle. I promised him I would do so. Our discussion was becoming uncomfortable, so I extended my pleasantries and left his office.

Later, while in the shower at home, I recalled my conversation with Ben. I do a lot of my reflecting in the shower, by the way, where there are no distractions, just the calming sound of running water on my skin. It is like looking yourself in the mirror, ploughing into your soul, naked and vulnerable, with no one there but you. I spent half an hour contemplating what to do next as water poured over me. What was driving my decision? What was I ultimately afraid of? What price was I willing to pay for my beliefs?

You see, Ben had been sitting on a project that was costing my unit loads of money and causing his Organisation to lose funds as well. I found out he was doing it for selfish reasons, to make some of his cronies happy. They were benefitting from the delay. Since he was the budget owner and played his politics well, no one was calling him out.

I was young and energetic, and I wanted to leave my mark. I was pushing for change, but Ben wanted things to be left the way they were. "If it isn't broke, then don't fix it. I know people, Jane. I have been around these circles for over two decades. I don't think anyone will miss you much." With those words, he had indirectly threatened me that afternoon when we had our conversation.

By the end of my long shower, I decided to do what needed to be done to get the project unstuck, even though I risked his wrath. During the next few days, I spoke with other executives in Ben's Organisation, and they wanted me to do whatever I felt was right. But my boss was standing on the fence. He recommended that I think it through wisely. If my bet worked, he would support me, but if it backfired, he made it clear I was on my own.

Yes, it is lonely at the top when you have to make significant decisions, sometimes with drastic implications, and have little or no support, with no one to watch your back.

It wasn't long before I headed for a meeting with Ben's CEO. During the meeting, I spoke with a slightly shaky voice. I was unsure about the outcome. I explained what I thought was the right path for his Organisation without naming names. He knew where the problem was. Emails started flying around once I left his office. Back at my office, I sat and waited for either the bad news or good news. Was

I really going to lose my job because a client, who was making a bad judgment call, phoned my executive management to complain about me?

In the end, changes were implemented rapidly. We progressed and the project moved forward. It seemed like Ben had issued an empty threat. I continued working at that job for another three years, even after Ben left for another Organisation.

A new report on women and leadership by the financial-services company KPMG presents a somewhat counterintuitive finding: As women advance in their careers, they become less inclined to take professional risks. When women do take risks, according to the report, it's typically with the goal of earning more money, as opposed to getting a title bump. What's more, women are significantly more likely to take risks to benefit their team or their Organisation, rather than to benefit themselves. The report found that 69 percent of women were willing to ask to get involved in a project, compared to 43 percent who were willing to tout their accomplishments.[14]

Although this survey was done in the United States, your career journey as a woman will require standing up and taking risks no matter where you live. I guess both men and women experience this, but risk-taking is more difficult for women if they do not feel adequately supported at the leadership levels of their Organisation or if they feel insecure in their relationships at home.

Women and Career

A feeling of loneliness has crept up on me at various times during my career journey. When I was first assigned to a senior management role and became a line manager in Ghana, I was one of the very few female management staff heading one of the main business areas in my Organisation. In my region specifically, I was the only female in such a role. Don't get me wrong, it was a position I aspired to

[14] (KPMG, 2019).

for years. When I finally got there, I realized there were unexpected challenges that I faced as a female in such a role, professionally and personally, and I struggled to address them.

In some cases, although Organisations are willing to promote us based on our achievements from our previous position, they seldom remember to support us for new positions that will push our boundaries. Quoting the Peter Principle, "Managers rise to the level of their incompetence."[15] My take on this is that we can also be promoted to our level of incompetence. The Peter Principle applies broadly to settings in which the skills required to succeed at one level in the Organisational hierarchy may differ from the skills required in the next level, such as expertise in science, engineering, manufacturing, academia, or entrepreneurship (Baker, Jensen, and Murphy. [16] To some extent, I had to deal with a constant series of crises and minor annoyances that threatened my mission of being an effective leader simply because I was a young female leading a male-dominated team. However, my ability to solve these problems and take advantage of opportunities prepared me well for future leadership roles.

One of my main challenges was managing my young family along with a continuously demanding professional life. Two days before a planned business trip to meet with a major client in Singapore, my nanny quit. I've had to find alternative care for my children in the past but not under this much pressure. I reached out to colleagues and friends for help. My male colleagues found my situation strange because none of them had ever encountered anything like it. You guessed right; they had stay-at-home wives who handled such situations. My husband and I were high flyers living in different countries, and he could not take the week off to watch the kids. I was new to Ghana and did not yet have close friends in the country to reach out to.

---

[15] (Peter and Hull, 1971)

[16] (Benson *et al.*, 2018)

Being without a nanny to look after my kids in the face of an impending crucial business trip was a major crisis for me. At that point, my kids were my main priority. Thus, I ended up sending a colleague on the business mission while I stayed home to sort out my personal challenges.

> I noticed that some of the challenges I was experiencing may have looked simple or personal, but they had far-reaching implications for my job. I reached out to human resources to ask for some form of mentoring or coaching. Unfortunately, because I was not in a structured management or mentoring programme, my request fell into a grey area. The lack of a defined process to access the informal mentors I required to support me made it a tricky situation for human resources.

Quoting Melinda Gates, "When companies assume that the work of caring for a family and maintaining a household is getting done by someone else, it hurts everyone—but it hurts women and minorities the most. Women, of course, continue to shoulder more of the work at home, meaning many can't dedicate as much time and energy to their jobs, and some drop out of the workforce entirely. And minorities have less access to networks, mentorship, and resources to help them manage mounting responsibilities at work and at home. When women and minorities aren't able to dedicate themselves to advancing their careers, it holds our companies back. Research has proven that teams without diverse perspectives aren't as innovative or creative. And Organisations suffer, too, when employees—both male and female—have to dedicate so much energy to simply keeping their heads above water, instead of thinking of ways to create more value. That slows down economic growth and leads to less prosperity for all." [17]

Later that year, I was fortunate to attend a women's leadership programme offered by Harvard Business School. It was a personal investment in myself, and it was worth it. During this executive training, our coach advised me to be the solution that I seek. Because some of my issues were gender related, I was advised to seek out other women who had followed similar career paths, inside and outside my Organisation. On my return home, I started cold-calling female executives that had walked similar paths.

I observed that many other women developing their careers, making tough, unorthodox, and challenging choices, needed support as well. So I started a Women and Career session in my Organisation. Once every quarter, a senior female executive in my Organisation would lead a video conference to support participants with career advice by sharing her experiences or discussing relevant career topics. Presenters were open to questions after each session. The sessions drew participants from several other countries within the region.

Participants asked practical questions, and our presenters shared valuable and insightful career stories. Informal mentoring relationships started to emerge from these sessions. As the sessions grew, demand for them became unbelievable. The sessions evolved under the auspices of a nonprofit Organisation with the same name, which I founded, and I opened them up to external participants and presenters.

I say it is lonely at the top because you will experience some new challenges, and your current stack of tools might be inadequate for the next stage. Even your existing support group, like your friends, might find the challenges strange. My decision to take a promotion that involved relocating to another country was not welcomed by

[17] (Gates, 2017)

some members of my support system. Some worried about the effect of my decision on my marriage and family, while others raised concerns about the parts of my life that should be prioritized. Should we not always prioritize our families above career? What does that really mean?

The Missing Christmas

Sometimes the isolation and loneliness stems from a deep sense of guilt from having to make decisions, which might seem selfish. My decision to relocate to Ghana felt unpopular because no one in my close circle had had a similar experience. A couple of friends introduced me to people who had attempted similar journeys, though not exactly the same. I reached out to them, gleaning all I could from them. Most of these individuals were men who relocated with their wives. To better understand the impact my decision would have on my kids, I reached out to the spouses of these men to find out how they handled schooling, social activities, and even basic errands like shopping. At that time, I struggled to find another married woman who had taken on an expatriate position for herself and relocated to a new country with her kids.

One time, I had to work on a proposal that was key for the Organisation and strategic because of its impact on our business in Africa. On that project, I worked with a remote client who was based in a region that did not celebrate Christmas. In addition, the client had a workweek that ran from Sunday to Thursday. This happened during the Christmas holiday season. I convinced my family that we should cancel our flights for a Christmas vacation trip with another family. My family hardly saw me during that period, as I worked late into the night. The only time I spent a full day at home was on Christmas day, and I was so tired that I barely left my bed but for meals. I won the contract, but sometimes I wonder if I stole one Christmas away from the lives of my loved ones just so I could further develop my career. Was the price too high? If I have another go at it, can I plan better?

In my quiet moments of reflection, I question some of my decisions, especially those that were unorthodox. As a businesswoman, you will constantly need to juggle key aspects of your life that need attention. You will feel guilt from never understanding fully the impact on your family, career, and marriage of the decisions you make. The struggle is real. You learn to live with some of the guilt because you may be unable to immediately share your feelings with friends and family. When you can share your feelings with others, it may seem that you do not receive the support required to move forward with clarity. It is a journey and all you can do is intentionally push forward.

Loneliness can be a strong word, and as we segue into the next chapter, I echo a quote from John C. Maxwell, "It's lonely at the top, so you better know why you are there."[18]

[18] (Maxwell, 2008)

CHAPTER 8

Women and Career

In the previous chapter, I talked about how I started Women and Career sessions in my Organisation and later developed the sessions into an independent nonprofit Organisation. I ran these sessions for about two years with my company at the time. Demand for the sessions grew, so we opened them up to women beyond my company and formalized them as a nonprofit. Q&As and career advice given by top female executives in these sessions are available on our social media platforms and our website, womenncareer.com. The website also has practical tips, tools, and resources for career growth, and it is designed for women around the globe.

Where did my passion for supporting the careers of others, especially women, come from?

I Always Knew?

I have an old digital picture from a time that brings great memories. In that picture, I'm wearing what looks like an oversized black skirt suit with a cream shirt. Standing next to me is my dear friend, Clementina Saduwa "nee Uvieghara." We are both smiling and standing in front of a classroom. We must have been in our early twenties, and we had just finished attending a presentation at secondary school in Lagos.

At the time, we were undergraduate members of the Institute of Electrical and Electronic Engineers (IEEE), and we had joined a subsection of the group called Women In Engineering (IEEE, WIE). Clementina was the chairperson, and I was the secretary. One of the main objectives of IEEE, WIE was to encourage more girls to study science. During school holidays, we visited various secondary schools and made presentations to young girls, encouraging them to study science and follow career paths in the sciences. Once a year, we held large events that were attended by a number of schools. The schools sent contingents of female students who participated in games, career sessions, and talks for the day. We wanted them to see science for what it truly is: a means to solve problems. And we wanted to discourage the notion that science was meant for only one gender.

I can't fully explain how my passion for this endeavour started. Clementina was a very good friend, and we had joined IEEE as a way to bring meaning to our lives. We enjoyed what we did, and the traveling made it fun as well. We were zealous. That was just how we both were—passionate about giving our best in whatever we did. Starting Women and Career did not seem like a lifelong dream or a deliberate vision, but in hindsight, it seems like a trajectory that I was destined to make. Retracing the dots, I see that the signs were always there.

In 2007, Clementina was killed in a random act of robbery in Lagos. She was on her way home from work. We both worked for the same Organisation while studying for master's degrees at the same school. Our commuting route was similar, so it could have easily been me on that fateful, tragic day. Clementina and I were like sisters. She was only twenty-nine.

After her death, I did not want to volunteer or be involved in any initiatives that encouraged girls to study science. I said no to travel and any speaking engagements or presentations outside work. Shock and fear sent me grieving for years. Subconsciously, I was running away from all that reminded me of Clementina.

As I've previously mentioned, in 2014, I attended a leadership course at Harvard Business School. Each morning before the main session, we met for board advisors' sessions, which lasted two hours. The board of advisors group consisted of four participants and a Harvard-appointed facilitator. The facilitators were Harvard alumni and registered executive coaches or management consultants in private practice. These individuals held senior roles, with many holding directorships on a range of boards.

During the sessions, participants shared their strategic plans, using a prescribed format, and gradually unpacked issues and opportunities. The group offered advice on ways to address each strategic challenge. Participants then developed and ultimately presented an action plan that could be implemented at work. When one particular facilitator was trying to unpack my purpose or passion in life, he asked me about the greatest fear preventing me from living the life I wanted. What would I do if I had no barriers or nothing holding me back? In that instant, I realized that one of my greatest passions was supporting other people in their endeavours—young girls, young men, career women, and others. I wanted to help ensure that they never stopped living a life of fulfillment, unlimited by what anyone thought of them. And yet I was running away from doing that. Why?

To my utter shock and amazement, I broke down in uncontrollable tears. I had lost a dear friend who shared my passion, and it scared me. I could not understand her death, and that made it difficult to go back to that life. For years, I lived what I considered a safe life, never wanting to give anything extra to this world. I thought that sharing my gifts exposed me, making me vulnerable, and I wanted to be safe. After the difficult session that morning, I made a commitment to follow my passion, though afraid of what the journey might entail.

Now having lived four decades and recognizing that many others might never develop clear ideas regarding their purpose in life, I feel privileged to have this awareness. For many people, that search is like a journey: The more we experience and know, the closer the end seems. While working on my fears, I redefined what a good life means to me. It is best summarized in a book I just finished reading, *Road to Character*, by David Brooks: A good life is a life that goes beyond creating résumé virtues (a great career) to building eulogy virtues. In other words, a good life is one in agreement with the things that I want to be remembered for. It is living my daily struggle to remain centered on my faith, to be a true wife to my husband and a great mum to my kids, and to inspire those who cross my path while enjoying the career I chose.

Where Are the Sponsors and Mentors?

I am a firm believer that your career journey is not a case of them against us. It is not a war between the sexes. As discussed in earlier chapters, my greatest sponsors have been men, and most of my mentors are male. We try to promote this idea during our Women and Career events and activities.

I would like to draw a slight difference between mentorship and sponsorship. Mentorship and sponsorship can both be formal programs designed by Organisations or informal relationships built by individuals, but the goals of each are different.

> Generally speaking, mentors provide advice and career guidance, but they may not be in a position to influence your career prospects directly. They cannot get you promoted, get you interesting projects or deals to work on, or get you seen by management. The goal of mentors is to provide a sounding board and some coaching. By contrast, the goal of sponsors is to help you advance in your career. A sponsor is someone who is in a position to influence your career opportunities and be a champion for your career advancement. Sometimes, the same individual can play both roles.

I am aware that Organisations may have difficulties managing issues regarding the perception of "unfair" advantage if women alone are part of the sponsorship programmes. However, in most fields or industries, men have historically been able to develop these relationships organically, whereas women have not. Hence, formal sponsorship programmes are not necessary for men. Nevertheless, the advice and support of mentors and sponsors can benefit both women and men seeking to advance their careers.

A nun once told my class in secondary school, "Every human has their good parts and not-so-good parts. Be interested to learn from the good parts." I have always approached mentoring from that angle, realizing that my mentors are not saints. In some cases, I am not seeking to learn from every part of their lives because they, being human, likely have parts of their lives with which they are struggling.

Looking back, I can say that mentorship is sometimes overrated. I have learned that good mentors in one area of your life do not necessarily translate to perfect mentors in other areas of your life. My first formal mentoring relationship almost blew up in my face when I thought a career mentor could also be a mentor in my marriage. We are complex beings. You are responsible for defining the aspect of your life that you want mentors to support. Always remember that you are the driver of the relationship, so make time to define the goals of each session and show up prepared.

They say that experience is a great teacher. But why learn only from your experiences and mistakes if we have people who have gone before us that can share their experiences. Never be afraid to seek out mentors and even sponsors. You never know how lucky you may be. Mentorship is a journey, and as you grow along the way, you might not immediately see the relevance of some relationships. Always give back what you have received, and learn to mentor others too.

My TEDx Speech and the Speech I Never Gave

In 2017, I gave a TEDx speech in a community called Ho in Ghana. My audience for the session was a university community of young students. Weeks before my presentation, I struggled with the theme of my message. In a conversation with my career coach, I insinuated that I was struggling with what I really wanted to pass across to the audience. She suggested I think back to my younger self. She said, "What would you like to say to your younger self?"

In the end, an article I wrote on LinkedIn, "The Speech I Never Gave," became the premise and title of my TEDx Ho talk. The article was written to express the conflict I faced in trying to justify some of my core beliefs about equity and justice—the need to have women supported in corporations.

The background for the article and the TEDx speech was an award ceremony for graduates that I had attended. It was the third year that my company was sponsoring the award for best graduating female engineering student in that university, and I was my company's representative. Sitting at the table with fellow sponsors for various other awards, I felt the buzz and energy as I scanned the room bustling with chatting students, who were mostly the recipients of the awards. It was a day to celebrate them. We were in the Great Hall of the University of Ghana. From the sea of black suits at the various sponsorship tables, you could tell that this section was filled with men who were corporate management representatives or lecturers.

After we introduced ourselves at my table, one of the lecturers enquired if my company could also sponsor the best graduating engineering student, who happened to be male that year. Apparently, the best graduating female engineering student was receiving more awards from sponsors than this overall best student was. My colleague looked straight at the lecturer and said, "Jane is the driver of this award within our Organisation; you will need to convince her." While the lecturer tried to make a case for the best graduating student award, I mumbled something along the lines of, "We can consider that next year. For this ceremony, we are focused on the best graduating female engineering student."

When I got home, I sat down and reflected on the events of the day. What was the essence of the award? Were we being biased by focusing only on female students? Had I allowed my predilection for female science students to influence this award? Should we sponsor both top male and female students? As I thought about these things, the reason I pushed for this award within my Organisation came back to me.

What I did not tell the lecturer at the table of sponsors was that I was rooting for Gifty Buah (yes, that was her name) because I could see my younger self in her. It was important that we encourage her because the journey she was about to embark on would require every ounce of support and motivation she could muster. I spoke with her after the event, and she shared her ambition of studying for a master's degree in engineering before launching her career in the field. I saw the passion and drive in her eyes, and I wanted to ensure that no one took that away from her. Yes, Gifty's journey to develop her career in the STEM industry required a fight.

> Charles Blow, an American journalist for *The New York Times*, once said, "It [racism] requires that you fight on two fronts; trying to reduce the size of the hill and climbing the hill." This captures how I have always felt about girls who study STEM courses and women who try to develop their careers and remain in STEM fields. We need to reduce the hill for women in this field because the rules of engagement were created with male folks in mind.

The *Women Matter Africa* report by McKinsey & Company notes that in Africa, women account for 47 percent of nonmanagement professional positions. At the middle management level, this figure falls to 40 percent, and at the senior management level, to 29 percent. This amounts to a "leakage" of 18 percentage points. I suppose that for STEM industries, the leakage would be even more. I do not have all the answers on how to level the hill, stop the leakage, and get more women in. However, I have decided to support all those women that I see climbing the hill. Honouring Gifty with the award was my way of passing the baton to her, and encouraging her to not let the hill stop her. I was fortunate that my company promoted diversity and the award was one that the Organisation sponsored.

To be clear, I have nothing against awards for the best students (including male students), but if, along the journey, Gifty decides to marry and have kids and not pursue her career, I wanted the award to remind her that she always had it in her. Pregnancy, should it happen, might slow her down, but it would not stop her from being smart. Should she start bearing kids at mid-career, I wanted her to recognize that the pace of her climb might slow down because of a couple of maternity leaves. She might have to work twice or thrice as hard to keep up the pace, and to give top-notch performances at work while no one cares that she spent most nights awake breastfeeding an infant or toilet training a toddler.

I wanted to encourage her to embark on a journey in which she might start off on the same pay grade as her male colleagues but discover eventually that the pay gap has increased substantially. And there may be people who suggest that the difference in pay must boil down to her negotiation abilities. A study by McKinsey & Company and Lean In suggested that women who negotiate are disproportionately penalized for it. According to the study, women who negotiate are 30-percent more likely than men who negotiate to receive feedback that they are intimidating, too aggressive, or bossy, and 67-percent more likely than women who don't negotiate to receive such negative feedback. Moreover, despite lobbying for promotions

at similar rates, women, on average, are less likely to be promoted than men. [19]

That, in essence, was the speech that I wished I had given to the lecturer and to all those who thought Gifty might have been overly patronized for her achievement.

For every Lucy Quist (the first female managing director of a telecommunication company in sub-Saharan Africa), there are many more just like her who gave up along the way because the hill seemed too steep and there were no cheerleaders to keep them moving. Greater diversity in male-dominated fields helps to bring perspective—a different way of looking at and solving challenges and old problems. Research shows that companies with a greater share of women on their board of directors and executive committees tend to perform better financially.[20]

[19] (Krivkovich *et al.*, 2018)
[20] (Catalyst, 2004)

I may have unintentionally missed the opportunity for this speech on that fateful day, but I have come to acknowledge why the award was so important. It was a reminder that for many females in the workplace, the challenge is no longer access but equality, as I've previously stated. Women need to be given equal consideration when it comes to opportunities, promotions, hiring, pay increases, and line management positions.

The great thing about sharing this speech here is that I get to share it with a larger audience than at the award presentation. We can advance the conversation on how to retain women within STEM industries. I am hopeful that readers will go back to their workplaces and start having these discussions.

I want to be hopeful—I want hope for my daughter so she can aspire to be the truest form of herself without the limitation of gender. This emphasis on my daughter's future became the last lines of my TEDx presentation. [21]

My company offered Gifty an internship after her graduation, but she opted to work as a graduate assistant with the University of Ghana. She said that citing the award on her CV demonstrated her ability to achieve excellence in her chosen field. She believes that the award influenced her success in getting a scholarship from the Mandela Institute for Development Studies (MINDS), and that it was instrumental in securing a place at Carnegie Mellon University, Rwanda, to study for her master's degree in wireless communication. MINDS, founded by Nkosana Moyo, is a scholarship programme that enables African students to study in an African country other than their home country.

I am very proud of Gifty Buah, and I still keep in contact with her.

[21] (Egerton-Idehen, 2017)

CHAPTER 9

Friends Incorporated

Mavuso looked regal as he ate his breakfast. He pretended to be oblivious to the fact that we came to see him. He did not bat an eyelid to recognize our presence, but you could tell from his side glance that his large ears must have heard our chatter. I stood and stared at him, with a sense of awe and of great respect. The story of how Mavuso came to Pilanesberg in South Africa is my metaphor for the importance of support during a career journey.

The Story of Ayo

In the early days of my career, I was fortunate to have met Ayo Arogbo in my local church. He was many years older than me and worked in the financial sector. With more experience and wisdom than my younger self, who was seeking to carve a career path, he became a mentor. He guided me in financial matters, including how to save and invest, set goals, and plan. I learned how to develop my personal mission statement and invest my resources toward personal development. His mentoring was as tactical as reviewing my university application forms and strategizing with me on how to get into MIT for a master's degree. When I needed the psychological comfort of a role model, he and his wife gave me their shoulders to lean on.

Life will frequently throw you out of your comfort zone, and so we grew apart after I got married. As I evolved, however, I used the tools and values that I acquired under his tutelage. I depended less on him and more on my own ability to seek a path for myself.

The story of Ayo in my life is like that of a matriarch elephant and her calves. The calves are breastfed and taken care of until they grow up and become teenagers, then they are pushed out of the herd. Once out, they seek other teenagers and form a new herd. The members of the herd support each other, playing and hanging out in the wild together.

Nne: Friends, Sisters, and Mentors

My metaphorical herd are the beautiful sisters who have become my core support team for over fifteen years now. We all lived in Lagos and met on the job. We were in the same telecom industry but worked for different Organisations. They are mirrors who show me a reflection of myself at each stage of my journey, and they choose not to judge me because they realize that I am a work in progress. They recognize that the reflection in the mirror is open to change with time.

One morning in March, at around 3 a.m., my thoughts came together, and I realized that my boss was trying to get me sacked. My husband was participating in a master's programme in the United States and was in his class and learning at that moment. But I knew whom to call. I went into my bathroom and placed the call because I knew instinctively that Nne—my good friend and sometimes advisor—would answer. My relief and mixed emotions came out in light sobs, which became cries as I tried to explain why I called. She kept repeating, "Nne, are you alright? Nne, did we lose someone?"

Nne in the Igbo language means mother, but it has come to symbolize the nurturing instinct of any woman. Women call each other Nne because the meaning cuts deeper than friendship. It symbolizes our roles as friend, sister, coach, and mentor. It took a while for me to explain why I had called. I had been having weeks of hell at the office as I faced one disciplinary panel or the other. What started as a mini-investigation into my personal assistant's role in planning a party ended up being a full-blown investigation that questioned my actions vis-à-vis the company's values. It was so unreal, and it took me time to recognize that it had blown out of proportion. My girls were aware of what was going on, but that early morning was different. I finally realized that my most trusted boss was the one who stuck the dagger deep while looking into my eyes.

An hour later, after my conversation with my friend, followed by a prayer, I returned to my room where my son was sitting up on my bed.

"Mum, why were you crying in there?"

I was shocked. I did not realize that my crying had woken him up. What was I expected to explain to my nine-year-old son? Emotions ran through me as I quivered. "Asher, don't worry. Someone I trusted at work disappointed me. He did something that really hurt me."

His eyes asked for more details, but I had zilch emotional capacity to explain further. He said, "Okay," accepting my vague explanation as I walked into the living room. I needed somewhere I could cry in peace.

That was my first experience with corporate politics gone wild. My company was having serious cash flow issues. We had lost a huge portion of our market share globally. The Organisation was seeking ways to reduce cost and remain nimble. The signs that the boat was rocking were there for me to see, but I figured that since my company had been in existence for over a century, we could figure things out. My department was doing very well, and I was exceeding my targets year after year. What more did I need to do? I thought my boss was proud of me. But when I eventually found out that he was actually trying to get me fired, I resigned. I didn't think I could work with a deceptive person like that.

I was never one to dig deep into what was happening in top management. I was there to do my job as best as I could. Everything finally made sense when two days after I resigned, it was announced that some restructuring was being carried out, and everyone at my boss's level had been made redundant. Well, my role was now vacant, and my boss had struck a deal to take it over so that he could stay within the Organisation.

For weeks after my resignation, I depended on my support system: my husband, my core sisters, and the team of excellent friends I had made. I needed them all to help me make it through the uncertainty and emotional journey ahead. For the second time in my life, I wanted to shrink away and disappear. The thought of being betrayed made me seek closure, and I started writing. The stages of grief were playing out in my life, and I felt like a mother abruptly weaned away from her baby. Writing about my experiences as a career woman was therapeutic, and those writings gave birth to this book.

Seeking Support and Embracing Friendships

Like a young elephant thrown out of a breeding herd and seeking to move with a new group of other young elephants, I have always sought support among ladies who, like me, are seeking to develop their careers. When I relocated to Ghana, I decided to make acquaintances with women outside my Industry to explore new grounds.

This decision opened me up to Phyllis. Our friendship started when she complimented my shoes at church, and we then found out that our kids attended the same school. After some coffee and lunch dates, it became clear that she shared my core values and had the drive I so admired. She worked in the financial sector, having relocated to her native Ghana after working for Goldman Sachs in the United States. Phyllis was a connector, and she introduced me to Hilda, Akovi, and Kemi, who completed my herd of teenage elephants. They were all amazing women who were working out their careers and family life. In their company, I was challenged, while I also had fun and permission to dream. On some Friday evenings, we hung out by the bar in my apartment complex as we discussed marriage, kids, goals, and dreams. There was no need for competition, as we celebrated each other's successes and gave support when needed.

One weekend when I needed to make a tough decision, I spent Sunday with Hilda and Akovi amassing the strength and courage to make a bold move. Hilda's husband offered to take our kids out so we could spend quality time together. I dosed off in the salon while my girls got their hair done, and afterwards we went back home. Hilda is a wonderful cook. She served fried yam and *shito* (a fried sauce) as we shared childhood stories. Although no one discussed my decision as we talked about our childhoods, I found the motivation to make the move. That was all I needed—a reminder of where we had come from and the leaps we had made. To see little girls' dreams grow beyond their imagination, as reflected in my friends, gave me courage to walk into the unknown.

Your support system can vary. Be open to receive support from friends and peers. They can give you the psychological and emotional support you need in times of crisis.

Mavuso the Role Model

The story of Mavuso and the safari in Pilanesberg is a story about discipline and discovering the value of experience and the wisdom in following a formula that works. In the early 1990s, Kruger Park in South Africa had too many elephants and initiated a culling and relocation program. That was why a breeding herd of elephants was taken to Pilanesberg Park to start a herd there. In the new park, as is normal with elephants, the mother cow took care of the calves until they became "teenagers." Then the matriarch pushed them out of the herd. The young animals banded together to wander the wild, playing with and supporting each other.

Unfortunately, after a while, the Pilanesberg rangers observed that the elephants were acting strange. While in musth, the males were killing rhinos. During musth, bull elephants go through a phase of heightened hormone levels, leading them to search for females to breed with. Musth can result in more aggressive behaviour and shorter tempers. My guide claimed that the elephants tried to mate with the rhinos and killed them if they refused. The band of young males had killed over forty rhinos by the time the park decided to investigate. The park officials brought in specialists and behavioural zoologists. Their findings suggested that the males were in a state of musth at a younger-than-usual age, causing them to try to mate before they knew how. The officials decided to introduce some mature male bulls from Kruger Park to "teach" the young bulls. That was how Mavuso came to live in Pilanesberg. He was one of the three mature male bull elephants introduced to Pilanesberg.

According to park ranger and field ecologist Gus van Dyk, "One of the lessons from the entire situation is that the role of the male elephant is a critical one, particularly in what has been traditionally viewed as the matriarchal society of an elephant herd. Mavuso and the other Kruger males showed that it is only through a no-nonsense approach that they could restore the equilibrium of the herd."

Without the older role models to teach them the ropes, the younger bulls were behaving badly, bullying females in their awkward attempts to force them to mate. With the larger, stronger, older elephants around to teach the youngsters correct etiquette, the musth cycles of the youngsters returned to normal, and the incidents of rhino killing—as well as tourist vehicle attacks, which had also been a problem—were greatly diminished.[22]

The story of Pilanesberg and the introduction of Mavuso and other adult bulls is one I hold close to my heart. I have realized that while walking on this journey, we need role models, mentors, or the support of older, more experienced persons from whom we can learn. I find them in Magnus, Africanus, and Raphael—some of the male mentors who have supported my journey. I intentionally seek

---

[22] (Leontsinis, 2015)

mentors who are male or female, including business or corporate colleagues of either gender that I can learn from. Some mentoring sessions are structured; I spend time with them once a quarter or reach out to run an idea by them. Other sessions are as informal as stopping by for family dinners and experiencing their leadership in their homes. They may live in different countries and continents and may not be perfect people, but there are certain areas of their lives in which their strength, wisdom, and grit have made them standout as outliers and value creators.

Meanwhile, as Mavuso continued to eat his breakfast, a calf from a nearby herd tried to get his attention. Mavuso was quick to put him in his place. A loud trumpet call sent the calf running for his mother. The morning sun was rising and the sunlight across the grey rumpled skin of the animals was a beautiful sight to behold. Mavuso had an important task—to teach the youngsters about their surroundings and educate them about what they could eat, what they should avoid, and how to be an elephant.

Ayo Arogbo was the Mavuso I needed in the early days of my career. Ayo taught me skills and exposed me to resources I needed as a newbie starting a career. It was much like the older elephants showing the younger elephants how to behave, how to eat, where to go for food, what was safe, and how best to navigate their surroundings. Transitional points in your career, such as moving to a line management position or executive level, require similar guidance and support.

These days, many companies are trying to create this form of mentoring or coaching support for staff. In some cases, this may be done via a line manager, while in other cases, a senior colleague may be assigned to the staff. Managers are sometimes limited in the type of support they can offer. Some can help only with information that relates directly to the activities of your daily routine work. They do not offer personal developmental support. In such scenarios, you may want to directly approach a senior colleague who is well seasoned to guide you on a development track, or you can seek the services of professional career coaches if you can afford one.

The support system provided by male and female mentors is imperative to achieving balance. You may alternatively need coaching, mentoring, and nurturing support. There will be times when you need discipline and accountability. Never belittle the importance of having role models like Mavusos in your journey because your journey will require them. Seek them and embrace them. I would advise you to seek role models both within and outside your industry. These types of relationships can provide you with valuable information and personal development resources; they can help define a sense of purpose for you; they can advocate for appropriate work-life balance; and, they can offer developmental feedback.

Field ecologist Gus said, "I think everyone needs a role model. These elephants had no role model and no idea of what appropriate elephant behaviour was." I agree with Gus, especially when we are seeking a career change or moving into new responsibilities at work.

CHAPTER 10

Giving Yourself Permission

Mama Ku Ukwuu (grandmother) was what my father sometimes called me. To him, I was his mother reincarnated. As my lanky limbs, knock knees, and physical build formed, I began to look like her. Dark skin, high cheek bones, oblong face—the similarities were there. As a young adult, I began a search trying to discover who I was. The initial goal was to discover my strengths, in the hope that I could use them to progress my career. Over two decades later, the search for who I am continues.

My Fortieth Birthday

On January 9, 2017, I celebrated my fortieth birthday. I had long wondered how I would celebrate this milestone. Unfortunately, my husband was out of town that week for business. I googled what others had done to celebrate their fortieth birthdays. After hours of unsatisfying searching, I finally decided to do something original and different, with no apologies. My coach had always talked about *being*, living in the moment and letting the river flow where it will. I struggled with that concept, as I always seek to control, plan, set goals, and manage every situation or outcome. In my subconscious, I had connected *being* with being bored.

I took my birthday week off to do things I have never done and in my own way. This was unusual in itself because the only time I take a week off is for family vacations. For my birthday week, I wanted to do the simple little things that have always escaped me, things I called trivia. I set absolutely no predefined goals, no matter how hard that would be for my controlling personality, so I could wake up each day with an unclear itinerary.

The entire week, I took my kids to school every day. On day one, I had coffee with school mums after the morning school run. During the coffee, I started getting bored listening to conversations about where to get the best vegetables and what the teachers were up to. That's when birds chirping close by caught my attention. It was refreshing to know that listening to birds could be so peaceful. Was this a glimpse of the mindfulness concept that my coach had always talked about? Later, as birthday gifts swamped my house, my husband called to send his love, and friends and loved ones called to wish me well. After that, I went shopping to get myself a blender (my birthday gift to myself, as I am into healthful eating), and I went to the salon to get my hair done.

Day two worked out pretty much the same, but I stayed a little longer at my daughter's school because she wanted me to watch her swim. I was glad I did that. Later that evening, while we were all home, I stepped outside for thirty minutes and watched the sunset. It was a beautiful experience. It reminded me that as kids, we cherished this fun activity. When I got bored later at night, I phoned some friends to catch up with them. This was not my usual routine. Mostly during the week, I am busy being a high-flying career woman chasing a project, as well as being a wife and a mum. I spoke with a dear friend who was going through a tough time in her career. I used to look up to her and was heartbroken to hear how demotivated she had become. I offered to do some research and connect her with possible options for a career change. I felt proud that I had gone out of my way to support someone I loved.

On day three, I took each hour as it came. The coffee mums at school offered to take me to lunch the next day. I thought it was a wonderful gesture since I—the busy executive—did not usually hang out with them. After school, my kids asked if they could play a bit on the playground before going home. I let them play for as long as they wanted, leaving when they were ready. They were chatty on the way home. I could sense that the extra playtime had made them happy. Watching them play changed my perspective about happiness. There was no need for candies, gifts, and all the fancy stuff I used to line up to entice them to stop playing on a normal day, when I was always in a hurry to get back to work.

I had lunch with the coffee mums after the school run on day four. We first spent time chatting over coffee. I was pleasantly surprised when they showered me with gifts and a cake. I couldn't believe this display of love! I had been so busy chasing my career goals that I had forgotten what simple living felt like. That evening, I went on a dinner date with myself, followed by salsa dancing. I love salsa, but it had been years since I danced. I refused to look at my phone during dinner. Rather, I soaked up all that was happening around me. Later in the evening, one of my close friends joined me, and we spent the rest of the night bonding over beautiful Latin music.

Day five was a continuation of my exploration of new or rare experiences. I went for a pedicure with one of the school mums. Then I spent the entire afternoon by myself, reading my Bible and listening to gospel music. I was beginning to enjoy being bored!

On day six, I went to my daughter's ballet practice. This had been a part of my routine for some time. However, while I waited for my daughter, I decided to tint my eyebrows and eyelashes, which was something new—and somewhat uncomfortable—for me. I was a little bit scared, but in the end, I couldn't tell the difference in my looks. Getting my eyebrows tinted seemed vain, but I gave myself permission to be vain for the day! I spent the rest of the day babysitting a friend's kids. She was out of town, and my kids love to hang out with her children. I even had time to do some laundry, which isn't something I usually do.

Day seven was *boring* as well, but boring was beginning to sound like fun to me. I invited my golf buddy to church, and he loved it. I couldn't remember the last time I reached out to someone for a social meeting outside my business circles. Then I went shopping for salmon and watched soccer on television. I hardly ever watch soccer. I would rather watch a movie. Frankly, I spent most of the time during the match anticipating the end. But I was getting comfortable doing uncomfortable things.

I celebrated my forty years on this planet by learning how to get bored. Yes! I had a boring birthday, one that opened me up to the possibility of just being. As a driven, goal-oriented, career person, I learned that it is okay to sometimes allow things to happen on their own. It's fine to simply live a bit.

Self-Awareness

A common thread that reoccurs in most of the materials on leadership that I have read is the concept of self-awareness (which we discussed earlier in this book in other contexts). Outstanding leaders are known to possess self-awareness because they have the ability to understand their values, their strengths and vulnerabilities, and their motivations—the qualities that make them tick.

In one of the Organisations I worked for, I started mentoring sessions for younger colleagues seeking to develop their careers. I paired them with employees from different product units. They learned new skills and information while being engaged and productive. At the end of each session, they had to make a presentation to the entire team and their coach. They were free to propose ways in which we could improve on existing issues. Some bosses might have found my actions irritable to the point of intimidation, but the Organisation began to experience the advantage of having young talent with enhanced skills and knowledge. The HR team became very interested in taking over the sessions.

My boss was opposed to the sessions. He probably saw this as my pet project, and he was having none of it. He wanted all eyes, especially mine, on the immediate goal before us, with no distractions. He was used to a strictly structured, top-down approach to training, and my sessions were too informal and different for him to accept.

During my undergraduate days, after reading the entire syllabus during vacations, I had held discussions with fellow students to ensure that I understood the concepts and all possible complex questions. It was a fun and very easy way for me to learn. By my fourth year, I was standing in front of a hundred men (there were only ten women in my class) to discuss and teach. I was fortunate to realize early on that I learned best by sharing and teaching.

I was also learning from the sessions that I organized in my company. My new position required high-level exposure to all of our different product portfolios. I would not have been able to read all the product information in the short time available. The sessions offered a quick way for me to get a good knowledge of our entire product portfolio.

My priorities and passion were different from those of my boss. Being a boss myself, I understood that you don't always have to share the same interests with your team or subordinates, even if that is one of your Organisation's goals. Although some people might use work as a platform to merge their passions, especially when work ideals align with personal interests, others might seek to express their passions only outside work. With my sessions, however, I was doing something for the greater good, which aligned with my Organisation's goal to drive diversity and inclusion, and it went way beyond my official duties.

I asked myself what could go wrong if, contrary to my boss's wishes, I continued the sessions. I might be sidelined by my manager or sacked. I calculated how much I had saved up, and it wasn't as much as I hoped for. My biggest fear if I lost my job was the impact it would have on my kids, and the disappointment my husband would feel. He would have to support me during a job search and probably wonder why I didn't think through the decision before walking away from my job, trying to save the world.

This dilemma drives home the importance of self-awareness. We should be aware of what we are willing to walk away from a job for, go the extra mile for, and die for. That core inside us needs to be nurtured, respected, and not suppressed. I am a fan of Marcus Buckingham's theory that each adult possesses a certain mix of fixed personal character attributes that make up our strengths—the things we should focus on. The alignment of our strengths with our actions creates a harmony when we bring our authentic self to work. Sometimes, your managers might not appreciate or acknowledge these strengths. However, if your Organisation's values or goals are not in conflict with your strength, I think you should stand your ground.

After much soul searching, I went ahead with my decision to keep holding my sessions, choosing my core and willing to face the wrath of my superior. With time, my boss got used to my "pet project," as he indeed called it.

Maybe we have all been at this point in our career, or in our marriage, partnership, or life in general. The dilemma of authority versus passion, or authority versus belief, forces us to look in the mirror and acknowledge who we really are. It tests our inner being: What would you do out of passion, no matter what others thought about you? Once you are convinced, can you say "no" to a senior authority? Self-awareness is what drives the ability to say no.

Self-Worth and the Impostor Syndrome

Deveena had been trying to get my attention for weeks. We had tried to book several virtual sessions, but they conflicted with our time schedules. Now we found ourselves at an industry-organized conference. We quickly rushed to a private corner where we could chat. She had so much to tell me, she said. She had started a new venture as a founding partner with two men. For some reason, she was beginning to doubt herself in the new executive role she was assigned. She could not come to terms with the fact that she was qualified for it. She needed mentoring because she felt that her skill sets were not good enough and that it would become evident soon.

I listened to her and acknowledged that her doubts are not uncommon for successful people, especially as they accomplish more and more. This is the impostor syndrome—also known as the impostor phenomenon, impostorism, fraud syndrome, and impostor experience. It is a psychological pattern in which an individual doubts his or her accomplishments and has a persistent fear of being exposed as a "fraud."[23]

I recounted a similar situation that happened to me a week earlier. I had been with about twenty-nine established businesswomen at Yale University. We were attending a training conference for women seeking board positions. I was so intimidated by the calibre of women in the room that I struggled to speak up for the first two days. However, when my mother called me on the second day to ask how I was faring, I told her I was doing great. She asked if I was there with colleagues or friends I had enrolled with, and I replied negatively. When she drilled further, I responded that I and a Kenyan woman were the only two Africans in attendance. Why I chose to frame my response in that way was baffling to me, but it was probably a reflection of how I felt at that point. I felt anxious that I was too young and inexperienced, compared with the other women in the room. I feared that they could all see through me and were wondering how I could have been chosen to attend this conference.

Interestingly, Joyce Roche was one of the coaches at the training session. An executive with over two decades of experience in the boardroom, she had written a book about this phenomenon titled, *The Empress Has No Clothes*. I recognized that both Deveena and I were experiencing imposter syndrome, a condition that was first

[23] (Langford and Clance, 1993).

described in 1978 by Pauline R. Clance and Suzanne A. Imes, both psychotherapists. According to Joyce Roche, this syndrome is the fear and self-doubt that causes people to question their abilities—even in the face of success—and to constantly search for external validation. Simply put, this phenomenon makes it difficult to recognize and celebrate one's strengths and accomplishments.[24]

Triggers for impostor syndrome happen when we feel different—for example, when we are in a group or situation in which we are different due to race, social and economic status, gender, or sexual orientation. We start supposing that the majority of people are making some kind of negative assumption about us, and we work like crazy to overcompensate for it and try to counter whatever makes us different. In that class of women at the Yale conference, whom I felt were far more experienced and accomplished than I was, my Igbo accent made me feel even more out of place whenever I spoke. Deveena felt different among her fellow executives as the only woman in the room.

Deveena and I were two very accomplished and qualified women, yet we still doubted ourselves in situations where we felt different. On the third day of my training, I discussed my concerns with my assigned coach (who was not Joyce Roche). She made me vocalize all my accomplishments that qualified me to be in the room. We even made a video of me pretending to talk about my accomplishments and skills to a room of imaginary listeners. During my classroom sessions, when feelings of doubt crept up on me, I would acknowledge the voice in my head and tell myself why I was worthy and deserved to be in the room. I tried to reframe my difference.

Joyce Roche explains in her book how feelings of self-doubt in high-achieving women or men can be managed. The first step is to talk to someone you trust, someone who can help you see what you may chose not to acknowledge (such as your achievements and

---

[24] (Simon, 2017).

skill sets). Then, the doubts can be conquered by internally validating yourself; analyze your strengths, not just your weaknesses. Additional steps include learning to accept compliments and other external validation, learning to show up as your authentic self, being aware that no one is perfect (especially in uncomfortable situations), and recognizing the strengths and vulnerabilities of other people.

In the words of Oprah Winfrey, sometimes we need to continuously remind ourselves that we are worthy because we were born. Never forget that you deserve a seat at the table.

Who Are You?

There is power in seeking to understand who you are. Sometimes it requires standing still, stopping in your tracks, and being present with yourself. My birthday week turned out to be a time to take a step back and nurture myself. I reconnected with myself, discovering what I love, what makes me happy, what I'm bad at, and what new things I can learn.

My altruistic motherhood and audacious career goals have always seemed like ambitions that drew from me as I nurtured others and kept going. The thought of caring for myself was a new concept. My fortieth birthday was my way of giving myself permission to care for myself and still be the ambitious mother and career woman. These goals are not mutually exclusive of each other. However, in achieving them, I am learning to look away and be confident with being bad at things that are not high priorities.

Two decades into this journey, I am still seeking to know myself. I am definitely not Janet Egueuka Amadi, my grandmother. Although my first name was derived from hers, her story is not mine. Janet was born an orphan and lost her husband as a young wife. She became a single mother of four kids—the fourth being the biological daughter of her sister, who died at childbirth.

In many ways, Janet's journey of discovery could be mine. She left the village for the city when she became bothered by male in-laws who tried to be intimate with her because she was a widow. She was unwilling to give herself to unwanted unions, even though the culture accommodated it. In her village, it was acceptable for widows to be passed on to in-laws for child rearing or remarriage.

She spent several years in Port Harcourt, a city in southern Nigeria, only to return to the village during the Biafran War, also known as the Nigerian Civil War. It was fought from 1967 to 1970 between Nigerian government forces and the Igbos, who sought to leave the country. During the war period, she had only one outfit, the one with which she had left Port Harcourt. Like other Igbos who fled the city for their villages during the war, she lost all the businesses she had built in the city. She was a businesswoman. In the village, she squatted with relatives but did not lose her voice. Instead, it became refined and confident. Her outspoken nature and no-nonsense approach to truth made her an influential member of the advisory board of the Eze (the Igbo ruling chief). This was seen as a laudable achievement for a woman of that time. The chief took her along when he was summoned to judge cases because he respected her wise counsel.

Janet set up the first Igbo women's group in her village, *aborigine*, to discuss community issues and solve social problems.. Janet was bold. She was a woman who most men admired, though some had a love-hate relationship with her.

My clearest memory of Janet is of her sitting in our living room in the village. I was probably four years old. My Mama Ku Ukwuu was this tall enigma of a woman, whose aura and authoritative way of talking allowed her to own every space she occupied. Sitting upright in a wooden chair, she insisted that my mum line our eyes with *tiro* before we left the house. Tiro, made of ground lead, is an ancient eye cosmetic used to darken and line eyelids to make the eyes pop. She was really into her looks. In one photo that I have, she sits majestically, looking at the camera with a confident smile, her neck and ears graced in gold jewelry. Her sleeveless blouse reveals well-toned muscles.

In many ways, I am Janet, a woman seeking to understand and own her voice, not afraid to be *bad*, and loving the vanity of life. Self-discovery is a powerful tool and a journey that might never end. It is one of the greatest gifts we can give ourselves.

CHAPTER 11

Tea with the Men

In this book, I have shared a lot of thoughts on some key issues regarding diversity, biases, and gender parity. If you are a man wondering what you are expected to do about this, the best response I could give was expressed by a male colleague who, after I had discussed some of the themes of this chapter, asked, "How can I help?"

When it comes to the concept of gender equity in the workplace, we hear various perspectives from men, ranging from "I don't get it" to "Merit is truly rewarded" to "There is no gender bias!" I would hope that the issues raised in earlier chapters shed some light on how both unconscious and conscious bias have been used to hold women back in their careers. But to men who still cannot understand, I urge you to be more curious.

Do not be blinded by the seductive nature of patriarchy. Patriarchy is a social system in which men hold primary power and predominate in the roles of political leadership, moral authority, social privilege, and property control. Some patriarchal societies are also patrilineal, meaning that property and titles are inherited by the male lineage.[25] When a social system benefits a few and promotes

[25] (Wikipedia, 2017).

inequality, there is a large chance it will not be sustainable. Do not be oblivious and insensitive to its impact on the population as a whole.

According to one school of thought, society is "meant" to be this way: Nature has created a societal construct that requires gender roles to be fixed and different for men and women. This is reflected in our family life, professional advancement, and leadership positions. It is the woman's responsibility to maintain the home and raise the children. The wife must give the husband's needs and wishes precedence over her own. Biology and nature made women suited for only supportive, nurturing roles.[26]

To those who subscribe to this school of thought, I would like to point out that data show that women can be just as ambitious, determined, and capable as men to develop their careers and take on leadership roles. In the 21st century, we see an increasing number of dual-career families, and we see stable and nourished relationships in which gender no longer automatically determines social roles. More women are finding equal employment opportunities, and more men are supporting them with domestic duties, such as baby tending.

In regard to the "How can I help?" question, allow me to share the following thoughts.

How Can I Help?

There was a scuffle at the gate outside his house and he could hear raised voices. The voices were familiar. Mazi Ogbonna headed in the direction of the heated exchange. He had to stop the loud, disturbing voices because he had a household of invalids to attend to. It had been a tough week for his household, with a couple of his kids infected with the dreaded sickness. "Ndi ebem gini na ese

[26] (Malkiel, 2016)

oku?" he excitedly asked the intruders, inquiring about the reason for the quarrel. He noticed that they had seized some of his belongings, and that Lazarus, his son, had been pelleting stones trying to stop them.

Mazi Ogbonna was informed that the group was there to collect the fines for missing "Uka Ukutu" (morning prayers). According to the doctrine of the Christian Missionary Society (CMS), members must attend the daily morning prayer service or be fined. He recognized the voices from previous prayer services. His excuses for missing these prayers were not accepted. Mazi Ogbonna and his household had been absent for days now. Most of his household were infected with measles, and someone had to take care of them.

Mazi Ogbonna was one of the delegates who traveled from Anara to Owerri to seek a pastor for the new CMS church in Anara. After a pastor was appointed by the church leadership to his community, Mazi Ogbonna walked the 30-kilometer journey back to Anara with the belongings of the pastor literally on top of his head. The entire journey took more than a day to complete, but he would later proudly recount this story to others because it was so meaningful to him.

Mazi Ogbonna was a member of the cabinet of Eze Agbugba, the head of the Anara community. He and other community leaders had argued that the introduction of missionaries to neighboring communities had brought progress in the form of education. During those colonial years, when a missionary pastor arrived, he usually founded a school alongside the church he established. Mazi learned about the importance of reading and writing after he conscripted for the Second World War, in about 1944. Nigeria, as a colony of the British Empire, was part of the Allied forces. As a new conscript, Mazi quickly realized that those who were educated were placed in higher positions. He was about to be shipped abroad to the battlefront before the war came to an end the next year.

Older now, a leader in his community, he was one of those pushing for the introduction and embrace of education. Contrary to some traditional-minded villagers, who were wary of education, Mazi sent all of his children to the new school established by the missionary. He even donated part of his farmland to the missionary. He never expected that his membership in the CMS would result in some nonsensical argument with other members.

As Mazi looked at the angry group at the gate of his compound, he realized that those individuals were not willing to accept reason. He asked them to leave and walked back into his house. They left. Bitter and vexed by the entire situation, he later took the matter up with the church leaders. Unfortunately, they took the side of the people who had seized Mazi's property as part of the fine. Apparently, these "leaders" felt the need to retain firm control or they lacked the boldness to challenge the status quo. As a result, Mazi Ogbonna banned the rest of his household from attending any more CMS services. Thus, he was not willing to serve this god because church members lacked empathy and common sense.

Mazi Ogbonna's vehement rejection of institutionalized fallibility is worthwhile to consider for those men who ask, "How can I help?" When it comes to gender equity and parity in the workplace, I would recommend speaking up when you see gaps. When you notice the bias and microaggression against your female colleagues, speak up and do something about it, at least by calling attention to it. That, for me, could be a first step in the right direction. In many industries, women remain in the lower levels of leadership and lack the power and range to speak for themselves without being punished for it. Power disparities and the range of acceptable behaviours for women at work can create a "gender double bind." If we don't speak up, we go unnoticed; if we do speak up, we get punished. That concept was fully explained by Adam Galinsky in his TED talk titled "How to speak up for yourself."[27]

[27] (Galinsky, 2019)

Underrepresentation results in diminished power and range to tackle problematic issues. In the workplace, the range of subjects that women can speak about without getting unduly punished by our colleagues is limited by our underrepresentation. This is especially true in cases and settings in which there are no laws protecting the victims and in which the victims have no social support or allies. Gender bias causes women to be passed over for promotions, to have their judgement questioned in their areas of expertise, to be expected to provide extra evidence of their competence, and to have demeaning comments made to them. These can be subtle but devastating workplace behaviors directed at women because of their lesser power compared with men. [28]

Sponsor Eligible Women

Women need sponsors, but most women lack one. As discussed by the Center for Talent Innovation in its *The Sponsor Dividend Report*, women need individuals ready to deploy relationship capital on their behalf in order to confer significant career boosts. These would be powerful individuals within an Organisation who invest the time to cultivate crucial relationships with female protégées who have track records of success. When they advocate for these rising female employees along all stages of their careers, their Organisations also benefit. Organisations that devote enormous sums of money to attract talented women would benefit as sponsors ensure that employers make good on their initial recruiting investment.

Organisations like to believe that they run meritocracies when it comes to promotions. However, numerous studies have shown that true meritocracies do not exist. As revealed in Christopher Mims' article on diversity, a technology columnist with The Wall Street Journal, managers tend to more favorably review employees who

[28] (Krivkovich *et al.*, 2018).

are like them.[29] Thus, the promotion of more men into management would likely lead to further male promotions and vice versa.

I have heard various stories from women who got a break into management because of the push or support they received from a male senior colleague. This is quite common in industries such as the technology sector, in which there are pronounced gender imbalances at the top. Consider the case of Gloria, a project manager in the technology sector in Nigeria.

Gloria had always found herself on teams in which she was the only woman. She was at the child-bearing and rearing phase of her life and had been passed over for promotions several times. The fact that she was a married woman managing a home was sometimes used as an excuse not to choose her, as well as to suggest that she should not be that ambitious. Also possibly working against her was the fact that she had been employed at a number of different companies, rather than a single Organisation. Women are more likely to advance to run companies in which they have had a long track record[30]. After several lateral moves with no clear career advancement, Gloria thought that her career had become stuck in a cul de sac, or dead end.

Gloria finally got a break when her senior colleague, who was well respected and influential in the Organisation, stood up for her. He took that stand in a meeting in which a role she had applied for was being discussed. She was surprised but grateful when she found out. She had begun to feel unwelcome in the Organisation. Gloria was seeking other options before she got this break. According to Mims, "The No. 1 reason women leave tech isn't a life transitioning like starting a family but the fact that they didn't feel welcome or

[29] (Mims, 2017)
[30] (Lublin, 2017)

included at their companies, in their teams or within the industry as a whole."[31]

I assume that most women at senior management levels would naturally advocate for and sponsor younger women. So the request here is not directed at women. The case being made here is the need for more men in senior positions to spend their political and influential capital in advocating for eligible women to move into senior roles. This is not a battle of the sexes or a matter of us-versus-them. This is a matter of pushing for gender equality and parity in the workplace. Research shows that companies with more diversity are more innovative and have better financial returns. This shows, in turn, that diverse companies are just plain smarter than their more homogenous competitors.[32]

In most industries and sectors, we still have more men than women at the upper echelons of the business or Organisation. To achieve gender parity and equity, we need people at the decision-making levels of these Organisations to advocate for women. We need male sponsors who are exposed to the work of eligible women to promote and advocate for these women. This would counter the current prevailing behavior of sponsors within an Organisation tending to select protégées who share their gender or race.[33]

A final factor to consider is the benefit for sponsors. Advocating for rising employees along all stages of a career can help to advance the sponsor's own career. Sponsorship signals one's leadership capacity to others in the Organisation—demonstrating that the sponsor is committed to the Organisation and tuned into up-and-coming managers.[34]

---

[31] (Mims, 2017)
[32] (Mims, 2017)
[33] (Center for Talent Innovation, 2019)
[34] (Center for Talent Innovation, 2019)

Support Your Wives, Sisters, and Other Women in Your Life

Sheryl Sandberg, through the Lean In Organisation that she founded, has described how men can best support the women in their lives and help them to thrive. Men can start at the home by truly committing to live as partners, contributing to their share of the household work, including child care. They can promote equity at home by encouraging their wives to stretch themselves in their careers. They can help model equality for their daughters by not letting stereotypes hold them back. Traditional girls' toys focus on physical appearance and caretaking, while boys' toys focus on competition and spatial skills. Parents should make sure that their kids play with a variety of toys so that they develop a range of cognitive and social skills. Fathers should encourage their daughters to lead, and celebrate them when they do. Fathers should also serve as role models for their sons, to help the boys understand what gender equality looks like.

Men can gain an interesting perspective on supporting women who aspire for career success when they try to see the issue through the eyes of their daughters. I received a revealing comment from a male executive regarding one of my articles about gender equity in the workplace published on LinkedIn: "*I have two daughters and I'm all for empowering women in the workplace and leadership roles. I want to see them succeed when they get to that point.*"

Work Has Commenced

How can companies best achieve gender parity?

In the context of gender equality, gender parity refers to the equal contribution of women and men in every dimension of life, whether private or public. Gender parity is often calculated as the ratio of females to males for a given indicator.[35] It is used as a metric for quantifying the representation of women versus men.

In September 2015, the United Nations General Assembly adopted the 2030 Agenda for Sustainable Development, which includes 17 Sustainable Development Goals (SDGs).[36] The UN SDG program seeks to create awareness and promote a holistic agenda that leaves no one behind on key issues. Achieving gender equality is one of the SDGs. Many Organisations around the world have pledged to promote and implement at least some of the SDGs. Evidence suggests that Organisations that take this matter seriously need to have buy-in and ownership at very senior levels for such programs to be fully implemented and effective within the company.

One way in which a company can ensure that it promotes gender parity and diversity and rewards merit is by committing to the systematic evaluation of its corporate culture, notes Aubrey Blanche

[35] (EIGE, 2019)
[36] (United Nations, 2019)

of Atlassian Corporation, an Australian-based software company.[37] Another way to promote gender parity is to set measurable gender representation targets across the various levels of management, including the senior level.[38]

In recent years, there has been an increasing realization that companies should train and educate employees about gender discrimination and unconscious bias in the workplace. Employees and line managers should be equipped with the information they need to ensure that they properly manage discrimination in the workplace, with the goal of eliminating it entirely.

There is still a lot of work to be done. Nevertheless, we are beginning to see positive impacts on various Organisations as awareness of this topic has been brought to the forefront.

---

[37] (Mims, 2017)

[38] (Krivkovich *et al.*, 2018)

CHAPTER 12

The Men's Roundtable* (*This chapter was written by my husband, Egerton.)

As soon as she walked in, the chatter in the room ground to a halt. She took her seat opposite the panel of nine, including seven men and two women. A senior manager of a top financial institution with branches in London and eastern, western, and southern Africa, she was about to be interviewed for a senior vice president position. She navigated the panel's initial questions with ease until they touched on the following subject:

"You know the role involves a lot of travel?"

"Yes, I do," she replied.

"As a married woman with kids, how do you intend to cope?" came the next question. "Are you sure you can do this job because of the travel? Can you travel as often as the job demands?"

And on and on the questions continued, with about 90 percent of the interview focused not on her competencies for the position, but on issues related to her status as a woman with a husband and kids. Very few questions were asked about her ability to intelligently strategize and execute a plan to move the company forward. She defended herself until she wondered if it might be easier to deny her status, that she has a husband and kids.

My name is Egerton Idehen. I am Jane's husband, and I am using this chapter of Jane's book to share my perspective—as a man, husband, and father—on some of the issues she raises.

My own career journey includes working as a general manager for the largest telecommunications network in Africa and the Middle East. In the course of my twenty-year-plus career, I have been the subject of several hiring and promotion interviews. I have also participated in many discussions about my career progress. My colleagues and bosses know that I am married with two children. Yet, there has never been any reference to my marital and family status in these discussions. I have never felt that a position for which I applied might be denied me because I am married with children. Perhaps this is not surprising, as I am a man.

I am a man who believes in women, and the overriding factor that shapes my ethos is the God in me. I believe that men are mandated to support and encourage women. In my actions, I have not always been true to this belief, but I'm putting forth a lot of effort to ensure that this is my reality.

Women who want to advance their careers face many obstacles. Any father, husband, brother, or male friend can see this. Even though this situation is gradually changing, I think a continuing major hindrance stems from legacy cultural norms regarding the mindset of women. By this, I refer to societal expectations of women, how women react to these expectations, and how women deal with the present realities of our modern world combined with the cultural baggage from the past.

Generally speaking, daughters from middle- and upper-class families in Africa are currently trained to be the best they can be. They are sent to good (private) primary, secondary, and tertiary educational institutions, often competing with boys for spots in coveted schools. Academically, at least, girls are schooled in the same manner in which boys are schooled. They study as hard as boys do, and they sit for the same examinations. As far as I know, separate entrance examinations for boys and girls do not exist. The engineering exam at university is not made easier for females to help them pass; it is the same exam given to males.

> However, after being exposed to this general gender equality during her school years, a woman is suddenly expected to discard her training or diminish her accomplishments at the altar of marriage and family life. This is society's basic contradiction—we first train females to reach for the stars, but we then saddle them with the weight of being a woman, which, according to traditional cultural norms, means stripping them of their personality so they can be led by a husband.

Identity Crisis

I recall once sitting with a lady friend and observing her looking at another woman who had achieved success in the corporate world. Without warning, she turned to me and said, "I was good in school; I was smart. Look at that lady up there." She pointed to the podium and then added, "I was better than her." Maybe these two women had attended the same school; I did not ask. But I heard what she was saying. She would have wanted a different life, but she had given up everything for her marriage and family. On the other extreme of the spectrum are women who have made a wreck of their marriage or who remain unmarried even though they desire marriage. Those women were not able to figure out how to balance family and career.

The belief inculcated in many women—either consciously or unconsciously—is that they cannot live up to their full potential. After training as a medical doctor and graduating at the top of her class, a woman is expected to abandon or relegate that amazing accomplishment to the background in order to accommodate marriage and family life. This dilemma raises questions in the minds of young women: Who am I? What should I do with my life?

A woman who doesn't really understand who she is might play to either of the two extremes I described above—rebel totally or conform fully. She may lose out from the benefits of being married and raising a family as she pursues her career, or she may capitulate and adhere to societal expectations while she loses her career dream and herself. Either way, it's an unhappy place for many women with whom I've interacted.

The problem amounts to a female identity crisis arising from a conflict in cultures—women's empowerment versus social traditions.

Nonbinary Choices

I often tell people that one of the biggest problems we have in Africa is that we've managed to gain one thing, but we've refused to let go of the other thing. Let me explain. Take our food, for example. In Nigeria, for the most part, our diet was historically suited for the traditional agrarian economy. Carbohydrate-heavy meals were necessary to fuel the physical exertion required in nonmechanized farming chores, such as tilling, digging, planting, watering, weeding farmlands, and rearing animals. When the wave of the Industrial Revolution hit our shores, we adapted to blue- and white-collar jobs that had more automation and less manual labour—but we did not change our cuisine. This cultural conflict, I believe, is a factor in the rise in cases of diabetes, hypertension, heart failure, and high blood pressure, among other pathological conditions.

In the same clashing, incompatible manner, we're encouraging our daughters to develop their mental faculties and compete with boys in school for the service of humankind and the enjoyment of their own lives—but then we later stifle that progress with outdated traditions and prejudices. We expose our daughters to Western-style liberal education, which inspires them to aspire for more. But we cling to our traditional roles in marriage, with the man being the lord who fends financially for the family, while the woman takes care of the home and raises the kids. The result is chaos and destruction.

> I believe that choices for women do not have to be binary—either this or that. I believe there is a healthy and fulfilling place of balance. The task for us as men and women is to find that balance. I say to women, "You can do both." It may sound simplistic, but I like to note that God gave women both a womb and a brain. The womb is to carry and bear seed, and the brain is to develop other aspects of who they are. To focus on only one part—say, using your womb without developing your brain—is doing yourself a disservice because all parts make up the whole.

It goes without saying that, in this context, part of the brain is also used for nurturing a family. But the other parts of the intellect and personality that want to excel should not be neglected.

I believe that not only is talent innate and God-given, but it is also distributed irrespective of gender. Giving in to societal pressure or the contradictions you feel inside is a disservice to humanity as well as to yourself. Stifling one purpose in favour of another reduces the value that humanity might have gained from your existence.

Overcome the Limits

In the corporate world, ambitious women are often viewed negatively. There are certain unspoken rules about the levels to which women can attain. Women are often asked, in an accusing manner, questions such as, "But you're already a manager. Why do you want to aim higher?" Meanwhile, male ambition is almost always applauded.

When I was growing up as a boy in Africa, the possibility of a marriage and family hindering my dreams did not feature into any conversation about my future life or career. Yet, these are the considerations that girls and women have to grapple with not only in Africa, but in much of the rest of the world. Western societies have made much progress, but there is still much additional work to be done. As evidence, just look at the ratios of men to women among top business executives in the West or even in U.S. presidential cabinets.

Women still have to prove themselves beyond the bounds required of men. Sadly, credit isn't always given to women who rise through the ranks. Salacious slurs and innuendos imply that there's a reason a woman succeeded, apart from her brains and hard work. Even more shocking is that such rumours tend to be peddled more by women than by men. Many women fail to give credit to other women of substance and brains, instead of aspiring to emulate them.

As pervasive as these cultural norms and prejudices are, the biggest obstacles that women face in developing their careers may be internally imposed self-limitations to their emancipation.

Years ago, a male friend began a relationship with a female colleague who had joined his company before he did. When the relationship began, they were at the same level. Over time, he became a supervisor while she remained at the same level. When an opportunity for a promotion to supervisor opened up, he encouraged her to go for it. He was trying to make her see that she should reach for the best she could be. But she seemingly did not care much about the position, and she did not get it. When they later started talking about marriage, they realized that company policy forbade both members of a married couple from working for the Organisation. The conversation as to whether he was going to quit never came up because she automatically assumed the role of the one who should quit. Before either of them could resign, however, they broke up. Thirty years later, he has now advanced to the position of executive director, while she has remained at the same level for the past thirty years. She is married to another man, with whom she has had children. She decided to prioritize her family life over her career advancement.

It is sometimes difficult to understand why a woman with a promising career feels that after she gets married, her spouse should take care of her. I am referring to the mindset that says, "I'm married, and the money I make is for me. Let my husband work and take care of me and the family." With this mindset, women put their careers in snooze mode. In some cases, both partners may start at the same level at work, but the woman chooses to bring zero aspiration to the union, while the man advances his career.

I have a female friend who graduated from university about two years before her future husband did. She started working and began to establish herself financially, while he later graduated and began hustling. After they were married, she lost interest in her career progress and devoted her time to praying for her husband's success: "Oh God, please give my husband money." It could come across abdicating; had she imbibed society's message of limitations and made it her own limitation?

The issue, then, is how do women overcome their self-limitations? This book was partly written to help women deal with this issue. I hope women who read it consider its points seriously. When I look at my wife, Jane, I admire the fact that she always felt that she was capable of bringing greater value to the family than only the roles of wife and mother. Marriage did not stop her dreams and aspirations.

How to Help

Nigeria is Africa's most populous country, with nearly 200 million people, half of whom are female. If 50 percent of society is limited and marginalized, then we are stifling 50 percent of potential innovation and creativity. In my view, beyond setting up agencies to promote women's empowerment and encourage diversity, which have often been pet projects of first ladies, government has to back up its talk with political will and action. On the positive side, many competent women have been and continue to be appointed to the executive cabinet in Nigeria. But the world is still holding up Rwanda as a model because its parliament has the highest percentage of women in any single parliamentary house [1](The UNWOMEN puts it at 64% after the 2013 elections)[39].

The Nigerian government is committed to the United Nation's SDG 4, to ensure that all girls and boys complete free, equitable, and quality primary and secondary education, leading to relevant and effective learning outcomes by 2030. That commitment is key because currently fewer girls go to school than boys. Education unlocks a world of possibilities, crucial for the prosperity of individuals and their communities.

Private companies need to make concerted efforts to bridge the gender gap, such as by enabling work environments in which gender bias is taboo. To me, the tougher task lies in the fact that all of us, including those formulating policies, have gender bias issues. We are all products of society. I can't even say that I am an exception. Realistically, this isn't something we can eliminate immediately.

We can start by formulating and articulating the right policies, and by understanding that even while exhibiting bias, people may mean well. Take the case of the interview I mentioned earlier. Some of the panelists might have based their seemingly biased questions on their genuine concern about saving the marriage of the lady being interviewed. This brings me to another point. Regardless of how we frame the argument against gender bias, we cannot ignore the fact that, generally speaking, women tend to have certain characteristics, such as a nurturing instinct, that men don't.

Through training and coaching workshops, Organisations can begin to change people's minds. By celebrating diversity and encouraging women who have risen in their careers to mentor others, Organisations can take advantage of the innovation, skills, and

[39] (UNWOMEN, 2018)

unique talents that females possess. That woman who was overlooked might have the next big idea.

As for men, we need to realize that times are changing and begin to change as well. Men have put themselves under tremendous stress by thinking that they alone must provide for their families. They have been taught that their primary role is to provide, and they haven't learned to embrace a dual household income. Many men encourage their wives to stay home and not work, thereby creating a huge risk for the family's financial situation. Men tend to develop stress-related illnesses, such as cardiovascular disease, perhaps related to carrying the weight of the family's financial responsibilities and not acknowledging the need for help.

I used to tell Jane—maybe to force myself to shift my paradigm—"Well, if you start earning more than twice our salary, maybe I need to stop working. What's wrong with me staying home and taking care of the kids?"

I know that this type of paradigm shift is a particularly tough task for men in the African context, where traditional ideas still have a strong hold on society. However, I firmly believe that more African men need to encourage women to pursue their dreams and acknowledge the talents and abilities of women. The reality is that women can be better at some things than men, and this doesn't mean that men lose out. So, first of all, let's have open conversations about supporting women in this regard. Then let's consciously promote these ideas rather than oppose them. And let's also start celebrating women for what they are capable of doing and not just for their pleasing faces and fashion.

The Sponsorship Debate

In my mind, the truest case of a woman who has broken the proverbial glass ceiling would be someone who charts her own path that other women can follow, someone who has surmounted barriers and competed in the open market with peers, both male and female, and has won *without* the help of a sponsor.

However, I know that many men and women benefit from having sponsors who lend their influential capital to advocate for their growth and promotion. I appreciate the argument that because many women are starting from ground zero, they need sponsorship even more to get ahead. Nevertheless, I am concerned that women who rise through the ranks with the aid of sponsors run the risk of not being properly respected by their peers, as well as the risk of lacking credibility in their positions. Their narrative might end up being, "Yes, she's smart, but she was helped." This type of narrative could potentially demotivate other women from developing their careers if they cannot get someone to sponsor them. Another potential problem is that male peers might not validate the success of sponsored women because the men may feel that they were not beaten "fairly."

Thus, my advice to women is to not seek a special soft landing. Let people respect you for your demonstrated talents and capacity to grow. I realize that even when a woman is not being sponsored, she may not be given her due respect, and colleagues may question the reasons for her success. However, working to amass personal currency by being good to coworkers and investing in solid professional relationships with them will help women navigate the complex Organisational hierarchy. Men tend to build stronger bonds than women, especially in the corporate setting. I suggest that women could do the same.

Yes, the corporate world is a tough environment and the playing field isn't level, but if a woman hangs in there long enough and builds relationships, her internal capacity will come to the fore. But she may have to dig deep to overcome. There's no story more inspiring than rising in spite of all the odds. That, for me, is the ultimate accomplishment.

Last Card

Jane and I are introducing our daughter to activities that excite her creativity because we want her to bloom. I am a supportive father who strives to validate her based on her potential. I fail sometimes. I fall into old ways of thinking. When I think about asking her to go to the kitchen to learn to cook, I have to check myself. Do I want to tell her this because it is a female skill required for marriage or because it is a good life skill that everyone needs to learn? Sometimes we are very demanding of our son with regard to his academic work and not as demanding of our daughter. But when we realize this, we make adjustments to expose her to the same rigour required to excel. We are raising our son to respect women and see them as his equal.

We live in a world that has made a paradigm shift from marketplace to market space, where we don't have to physically go anywhere to transact business. Whether in Tokyo or South Africa, we are all buying from the same market. In raising our children to function in this new world, the last thing we want is for them, especially our daughter, to feel that their choices are binary. Jane and I are committed to modelling a healthy partnership between a man and woman, redoing our steps when we stray. After all, children are more likely to do what you do, rather than what you say.

Before I got married, I made up my mind that marriage was not an avenue to strip someone of his or her personality, but instead to enhance it. I'm convinced that people are happiest when they are living out their full potential.

As our courtship progressed, Jane and I spent an evening at what was arguably, at that time in Lagos, *the* hot spot for lovebirds—an entertainment centre called Silverbird Galleria. We were talking marriage and asking questions of one another.

Jane asked me, "So how do you see us in ten years' time?"

I replied, "Well, I'm working, have a great family—a boy and girl, a wonderful wife, a settled home—and I'm growing in my career." I then asked her the same question.

She replied, "I'm CEO of an Organisation, head of a board, launching this company and that company," and she added, "I have a family that is supporting me."

From that moment, I knew that if I was going to be all in, I needed to adjust my mindset to accommodate her strong and determined personality. I would have made her the most miserable person on Earth if I tried to turn her any other way around.

I knew that her response to my question that evening encapsulated who she is. Her career mattered to her. And I ultimately said, "I do."

CHAPTER 13

Closing Thoughts

Sitting at a table in a golf lounge after a game were a woman and a man. She was still dressed in her golf gear, while the man wore formal office clothes. As they chatted, she indicated to a waiter that they were ready for their orders to be taken. The waiter took their orders, addressing most of his questions to the man. He focused his attention on the man and avoided the woman's gaze—as if her contributions were inconsequential. The man became visibly uncomfortable and responded to the waiter, "You should be asking her. She's a member of this club. I'm actually the guest here. Can't you see that she's the one dressed in golf clothes?"

At that table sat Frank and I. Frank was my guest at the golf club, which I frequented. After the waiter left, Frank turned to me and asked, "Jane, do you get a lot of this? How do you handle it?" He was curious because he had two daughters in boarding school. In a light-hearted manner, I recounted a couple of similar incidents, noting that the way I handled them depended on the situation.

I continued, "Frank, getting upset with the waiter is not the solution. We can't educate him at this table today. His background, experiences, and perhaps religion might have taught him to view women from a certain angle. I have decided to take this problem to the level where more men can be educated—the level where our institutions can deal with gender equality on a daily basis. There, we can have more impact."

Frank leaned toward me and asked the question I would love more men to ask, "How can I help?"

That question is a good way to start for men interested in supporting gender parity in the workplace. I hope that from your reading of this book, you have gleaned ways in which your contributions to this issue can be meaningful and impactful.

> I encourage women to have tough conversations about gender parity with the men in their lives, especially the men who seem willing to understand. Knowledge can be a powerful tool, and having more men onboard means that achieving gender parity in the workplace and in society is only a matter of time. Let's do this for our daughters, who need to walk through their own paths to greatness, and for our sons as well. We owe it to them to make the world a better and more equitable place.

I started this book with stories about my first romantic relationship, my failed attempts to live up to expectations that didn't fit with my ideas of who I was, and my passive-aggressive reaction to the situation in which I found myself. I wanted these stories to help us consider the cultural expectations and presumed gender roles—both overt and covert—that are thrust upon women. These expectations and presumptions can set women up for career failure or cause them to give up on their aspirations.

I also wanted us to examine traditional corporate structures and how they are configured to favour males, along with why it is important for women to get a seat at the table and what they can do to make that happen. I wanted us to look at the intersection between career and marriage, including what marriage means for a woman's career and how it can make or mar her progress. I shared my journey of having children and described the impact this had on my career because I wanted us to address the structures and support systems needed to make a woman successful after childbearing.

My hope is that by considering pivotal moments in my career and examples from other women's stories, companies and other Organisations become more aware of how they can support women seeking professional advancement.

After reading the book, it should be clear that cultivating relationships and friendships and developing a tribe are important because no man or woman is an island. Such relational issues have become a backbone for most women navigating the corporate space. My personal experience with relationships contradicts the saying that women are their own worst enemies.

I do agree that, sometimes, internal obstacles hold women back from reaching their potential. This barrier needs to be broken. Discovering yourself and enjoying and embracing who you are is a key step in that regard.

In the chapter "Tea with Men," I make a case for more men to support and promote women, which I strongly believe can be advanced by sponsoring eligible women. I understand that not everyone is comfortable with sponsorship, as revealed by Egerton's comments in chapter 12. However, I know that for women as a minority group in the corporate world, this push to get more women at the table will go a long way toward achieving gender parity. I accept that we do not have to agree on every minute detail about how to get more males to support and promote women in the workplace. We can, however, agree that this issue needs to be addressed by putting all hands on deck and all possible options on the table.

In chapter 12, I shared a male perspective on the need for male support of gender parity in the workplace. It can be unsettling for some men when discussions about gender parity or equality are raised. Societal institutions, including religious ones, have sometimes made this a divisive topic because of uncomfortable and unsettling connotations associated with gender-related issues. Men need to have a safe space to ask about and understand these issues without fear of negative consequences. That could be a first step in bringing more men onboard.

To leave you with a final thought, the key goals of this book are to share insights from women who have sought to develop their careers while married; to empower women, men, Organisations, and institutions; and to discuss stumbling blocks to gender parity in society. I hope that you have found tools in this book to encourage you on your career journey.

About the Author

Jane Egerton-Idehen is the country manager in Nigeria and the regional sales manager for the West African branch of Avanti Communications Group PLC. Avanti, headquartered in the United Kingdom, provides satellite broadband and connectivity services to Internet service providers, mobile network operators, other satellite operators, various businesses, and government agencies in Europe, the Middle East, and Africa.

Jane was born and raised in Lagos, Nigeria. She graduated with a second-class upper degree in electronics engineering in 2001 from the University of Nigeria, Nusska. She furthered her education at Warwick Business School in the UK, where she received a master's degree, and she received an executive education at both Harvard Business School and Yale School of Management in the United States. She has worked in the telecommunications industry in Nigeria, Ghana, and Liberia for more than 17 years. Prior to working for Avanti, she worked for Nokia and Ericsson. Her knowledge of technology, her ability to manage complex stakeholder relationships, and her skill to manage teams and create strategies to support growth and drive business are keys to her success.

Being one of the few females heading key business areas in the telecom industry has exposed Jane to numerous professional and personal challenges peculiar to women. Spurred by discussions with fellow female executives around the globe, she organized a forum at Ericsson in which emerging and experienced female leaders could support each other in developing their careers. The overwhelming success of the forum led her to found Women and Career (www.womenncareer.com), to reach women beyond her Organisation and to support girls seeking careers after school.

Jane's passion for promoting girls in science, technology, engineering, and math (STEM) can be traced to her undergraduate days as a member of the International Institute of Electronics and Electrical Engineers (IEEE). Along with the late Clementina Saduwa (nee Uvieghara), she cofounded IEEE Women In Engineering. Jane has continued to be actively involved in speaking to girls and women about STEM careers. She has spoken at TEDx programs, the African Science Academy, Asheshi University in Ghana, and CFA's Start-ups Hangout. The latter program, founded by Chukwuemeka Fred Agbata, Jr., allows African entrepreneurs to meet, network, and learn so that their startups can excel. Jane has also spoken on several television programmes.

Jane does volunteer work for the ACE Foundation's Young Career and Graduate Mentorship Programme, and she is an aspiring fellow for the Aspen Global Leadership Institute. She was a board member of the Ericsson Diversity and Inclusion Board and of Moma Maternity, a retail division of Telfrent Solutions. A home girl at heart, she is active in giving back to the Ajegunle community of Lagos through the Sozo Network's #BeforeITurn18 programme, which prepares underserved teenaged girls for life, career, and leadership.

A quintessential extrovert and physical fitness proponent, Jane enjoys golf, cycling, and salsa. She also writes a regular telecoms column for *Business and Financial Times Ghana*. She and her husband, Egerton Idehen, have a son, Asher, and a daughter, Sarah, who inspire Jane to continue to push for diversity in male-dominated fields. Although she travels extensively, Jane continues to make her home in Lagos.

Jane invites readers to share their own experiences regarding adjustments needed for career women to succeed. The rules of engagement were created with men in mind, but women can succeed by creating their own paths through those rules. She hopes that we can all cheerlead these women to the finish line.

Visit her website, www.janeegerton.com, and share your ideas and experiences on how career women can be supported to grow. You can also learn how you can get career coaching support at the web site.

References

Aaker, J. L. (1997). Dimensions of Brand Personality. *Journal of Marketing Research*, 34(3): 347-355.

Alaka, A. M. (2011). Learning Styles: What Difference Do the Differences Make? Charleston Law Review, 5: 133-172.

Benabou, R. and Tirole, J. (1999). Self-Confidence: Intrapersonal Strategies. Princeton Economic Theory Papers, Economics Department, Princeton University.

Benson, A., Li, D. and Shue, K. (2018). Promotions and the Peter Principle. Quaterly Journal of Economics, Forthcoming. Available at SSRN, https://ssrn.com/abstract=3047193.

Casciaro, T., Gino, F. and Kouchaki, M. (2014). The Contaminating Effects of Building Instrumental Ties: How Networking Can Make Us Feel Dirty. *Dirty Networking Journal*. Electronic copy available at https://ssrn.com/abstract=2430174.

Catalyst (2004). The Bottom Line: Connecting Corporate Performance and Gender Diversity. Accessible at http://www.catalyst.org/system/files/The_Bottom_Line_Connecting_Corporate_ Performance_and_Gender_Diversity.pdf.

Centre for Talent Innovation (2019). The Sponsorship Dividend. Accessible at https://www.talentinnovation.org/private/assets/TheSponsorDividend-KeyFindings Combined-CTI.pdf.

Cohoon, M. J., Wadhwa, V. and Mitchell, L. (2010). The Anatomy of an Entrepreneur: Are Successful Women Entrepreneurs Different From Men? *SSRN Electronic Journal*. Kansas City, Mo.: Ewing Marion Kauffman Foundation.

Craven, B. (2019). Win or Die: Leadership Secrets from Game of Thrones. Webinar – Columbia Business School.

Dessy, S. and Djebbari, H. (2005). Career Choice, Marriage, Timing, and the Attraction of Unequals. IZA Discussion Paper. Electronic copy available at https://ssrn.com/abstract=692142.

Egerton-Idehen, J. N. (2017). Transforming Mindsets, Empowering Dreams. TEDxYouth@Ho Event. Accessible at https://www.ted.com/tedx/events/20622. European Institute for Gender Equality. Accessible at https://eige.europa.eu/thesaurus/terms/1195.

Elaina, R. (2003). Does Education Really Disadvantage Women in the Marriage Market? SSRN Electronic Journal. Department of Economics, University of Washington, Seattle.

Fineman, M. A. (2001). Why Marriage? *Virginia Journal of Social Policy and the Law*, (9)1: 240-271.

Fineman, M. A. (2008). The Vulnerable Subject: Anchoring Equality in the Human Condition. *Yale Journal of Law and Feminism*, 20(1): 8-40.

Galinsky, A. (2019). How to Speak Up for Yourself. TEDxNewYork. Accessible at https://www.ted.com/talks/adam_galinsky_how_to_speak_up_for_yourself/transcript.

Gates, M. (2017). We are Sending Our Daughters into a Workplace Designed for our Dads. Accessible at https://www.linkedin.com/pulse/were-sending-our-daughters-workplace-designed-deals-melinda-gates/

Gaudeul, A. and Giannetti, C. (2012). The Role of Reciprocation in Social Network Formation, With an Application to Blogging. Jena Economic Research Papers. Electronic copy available at https://ssrn.com/abstract=2088097.

Gladwell, M. (2016). Revisionist History Podcast Season 1: The Lady Vanishes. Accessible at revisionisthistory.com.

Gould, E. D. (2003). Marriage and Career: The Dynamic Decisions of Young Men. Department of Economics, Hebrew University, Jerusalem. Electronic copy available at https://ssrn.com/abstract=424361.

Jackson, M. O. (2017). The Friendship Paradox and Systematic Biases in Perceptions and Social Norms. Department of Economics, Stanford University, Stanford, California, USA. Electronic copy available at https://ssrn.com/abstract=2780003.

Jones, G. W. (2010). Changing Marriage Patterns in Asia. Asia Research Institute Working Paper. Electronic copy available at https://ssrn.com/abstract=1716533.

Keller, H. (1957). The Open Door. Garden City, New York.

KPMG (2019). Risk, Resilience, Reward: Mastering the Three "R's" – The Key to Women's Success in the Workplace. KPMG Women's Leadership, U. S. A.

Krivkovich, A., Nadeau, M., Robinson, K., Robinson, N., Starikova, I. and Yee, L. (2018). Women in the Workplace 2018. LeanIn.Org and McKinsey Report. Accessible at https://www.mckinsey.com/featured-insights/gender-equality/women-in-the-workplace-2018.

Langford, J. and Clance, P. R. (1993). The Impostor Phenomenon: Recent Research Findings Regarding Dynamics, Personality and Family Patterns and their Implications for

Treatment. Psychotherapy: Theory, Research, Practice, Training, 30 (3):495 – 501.

Lehrer, E. L. (2006). Age at Marriage and Marital Instability: Revisiting the Becker-Landes-Michael Hypothesis. IZA Discussion Paper. Electronic copy available at https://ssrn.com/abstract=912213.

Leontsinis, B. (2015). How Kruger Elephant Bulls Become the King of Pilanesberg. African Insider. Accessible at https://www.africaninsider.co.za/how-kruger-elephant-bulls-became-the-kings-of-pilanesberg/

Lin, M., Prabhala, N. R. and Viswanathan, S. (2011). Judging Borrowers by the Company They Keep: Friendship Networks and Information Assymmetry in Online Peer-to-Peer lending. Electronic copy available at https://ssrn.com/abstract=1355679.

Lublin, J. S. (2017). Women Make Gains Towards Winning CEO Job. *The Wall Street Journal.* Accessible at https://www.google.com/amp/s/www.wsj.com/amp/articles/womwn-make-gains-towards-winning-ceo-job-148665381.

Malembanie, N. K. (2014). Women's Rights in Africa: From Feminism to Reality. Electronic copy available at https://ssrn.com/abstract=2429404.

Malkiel, N. W. (2016). Keep the Damned Women Out: The Struggle for Coeducation. Princeton University Press.

Matsa, D. A. and Miller, A. R. (2012). A Female Style in Corporate Leadership: Evidence from Quotas. *American Economic Journal.* Electronic copy available at https://ssrn.com/abstract=1636047.

Maxwell, J. C. (2008). Leadership Gold: Lessons I've Learned from a Lifetime of Leading. HarperCollins Leadership, Inc.

McKinsey (2007). Women Matter: Gender Diversity, a Corporate Performance Driver. McKinsey and Company, Inc.

Mims, C. (2017). What the Google Controversy Misses: The Business Case for Diversity. *The Wall Street Journal.*

Misra, S. (2012). Implications of Globalization on Education. *Romanian Journal for Multidimensional Education*, 4(2): 1-15.

Nainar, V. (2013). Patriarchy in South Asia: Structures and Relations. Analyse and Kritik Magazine.

Peter, L. J. and Hull, R. (1971). The Peter Principle: Why Things go Wrong. New York, NY: William Morrow and Company, Inc.

Price, J. (2006). Does a Spouse Slow You Down: Marriage and Graduate School Outcomes. Retrieved on 15th July, 2018 from Cornell University, School of Industrial and Labour Relations site; http://digital commons.ilr.cornell.edu/working papers/147.

Ramakrishnan, R. (2006). Reforms in Teaching-Learning Environment Towards Greater Interactivity: New Roles of Facilitators and Learners. XII IDEA International Conference, Mumbai.

Ravichandran, K. (2009). Brand Cultism: A Study with Special Reference to "The Hindu". King Saud University. Electronic copy available at https://ssrn.com/abstract=1369318.

Sahu, S. (2008). Working Women and the Changing Dynamics of Family: The Concept of Matrimonial Home Today. National Law University, Odisha. Electronic copy available at https://ssrn.com/abstract=2354207.

Shuktziner, D. and Rabinovici, I. (2011). Human Dignity, Self-worth and Humiliation: A Comparative Legal-Psychological

Approach. Electronic copy available at https://ssrn.com/abstract=1964371.

Simon, P. (2017). The Empress Has No Clothes: An Interview with Joyce Roche. Huffpost. Accessible at https://m.huffpost.com/us/entry/us-3601497.

Sonnenfeld, J. A., Ward, A. J. and Mundt, T. (2007). Firing Back: How Great Leaders Rebound After Career Disasters. Harvard Business Review.

Stutzer, A. and Frey, B. S. (2005). Does Marriage Make People Happy or Do Happy People Get Married? IZA Discussion Paper. Electronic copy available at https://ssrn.com/abstract=375960.

Teachman, J. D. (2002). Childhood Living Arrangements and the Intergenerational Transmission of Divorce. *Journal of Marriage and Family,* 64 (3): 717 – 729.

UNICEF (2019). Education. Accessible at https://www.unicef.org/education.

UNICEF (2019). Girls' Education: Gender Equality in Education Benefits Every Child. Accessible at https://www.unicef.org/education/girls-education.

United Nations (2017). Goal 4: Ensure Inclusive and Equitable Quality Education and Promote Lifelong Learning Opportunities for All. Accessible at https://unstats.un.org/sdgs/report/2017/goal-04.

United Nations (2019). Education: Improving Learning Worldwide to Benefit Business and Society. Accessible at https://www.unglobalcompact.org/what-is-gc/our-work/social/education.

United Nations (2019). Sustainable Development Goals 4: Quality Education. Accessible at https://www.un.org/sustainabledevelopment/education/.

United Nations (2019). Envision2030: A goals to transfer the world for persons with disabilities. Accessible at https://www.un.org/development/desa/disabilities/envision2030.html.

Wikipedia (2017). Patriarchy. Accessible at https://en.m.wikipedia.org/wiki/Patriarchy.

Printed in Great Britain
by Amazon

19262677R00092